THE BLACK WIDOW'S GUIDE
TO KILLER POOL

THE
BLACK WIDOW'S GUIDE
TO KILLER POOL

BECOME THE
PLAYER TO BEAT

◈

JEANETTE LEE

and Adam Scott Gershenson

THREE RIVERS PRESS
NEW YORK

Published by Three Rivers Press, New York, New York.
Member of the Crown Publishing Group.

Random House, Inc.
New York, Toronto, London, Sydney, Auckland
www.randomhouse.com

Three Rivers Press is a registered trademark and the Three Rivers
Press colophon is a trademark of Random House, Inc.

Printed in the United States of America

Design by Karen Minster

Library of Congress Cataloging-in-Publication Data
Lee, Jeanette
The Black Widow's guide to killer pool: become the player to beat /
by Jeanette Lee and Adam Scott Gershenson. — 1st ed.
1. Pool (Game)   I. Title. II. Gershenson, Adam Scott.
GV891.L44 2000
794.7'321—dc21
                                                    99-046062

ISBN 0-609-80506-1

10 9 8 7 6 5 4 3 2 1

First Edition

To my dear friend and mentor Gene
and my greatest love, George.
I dedicate this book and my life to both of you.
JEANETTE LEE

To the women I love—
nurturing and wise, beautiful and kind.
ADAM GERSHENSON

ACKNOWLEDGMENTS

Thanks to George Breedlove for his love, insights, and patience with me during the writing of this book.

To Pete Fornatale and Basil Kane. Their faith in this project let me know that everything was going to be all right.

To Imperial International and Jay Orner & Sons Billiard Company, Inc., for their support and for letting me have all the best equipment at my fingertips.

To Lisa Merkin, whose original Jot-a-Shot program produced beautiful diagrams.

To Bob Carman, who helped me look inside myself and share it with all of you.

To all the photographers who helped capture my spirit.

To Amsterdam Billiards, where this book was born.

To Wayne, Debbie, and Clark Johnson for close critiques and zucchini bread.

To the Women's Professional Billiard Association and *Billiards Digest* and *Pool & Billiard* magazine.

To Adam Gershenson, for all the early mornings and late nights he spent getting to know me. And thanks to his mom, Judith, as well.

To everyone at Octagon Athlete Representation, especially Tom, Dre, Deb, Cynthia, and Amy, for taking care of everything.

To Larry York, Steve Durell, and Stu "Slowroll" Matana for helping me keep my game in top form.

And to all my fans, friends, family, and neighbors, thank you for your friendship and support.

J. L.

Many thanks to Basil Kane, whose sage guidance helped us arrive at Crown.

To Jack Kadden and Jim Roberts, first-class newspapermen from the *New York Times*.

To Pete Fornatale, who combined a sharp critical eye with remarkable restriant. He asked only for changes that truly made the book better.

To Boston Billiards, the best host anyone could ask for.

To my mother, Judith Rendely, who interviewed Jeanette one morning while I slept and later held the manuscript in her hands while I revised it with a red pencil and a broken wrist.

A. G.

CONTENTS

PART III
LIFE ON TOUR

It is not the critic who counts, not the man who points out how the strong man stumbles, or where the doer of deeds could have done better. The credit belongs to the man who is actually in the arena, whose face is marred by dust and sweat and blood; who strives valiantly; who errs and comes up short again and again, because there is no effort without error and shortcoming; but who does actually strive to do the deeds; who knows the great enthusiasms, the great devotions; who spends himself in a worthy cause; who at the best knows in the end the triumph of high achievement, and who at the worst, if he fails, at least fails while daring greatly, so that his place shall never be with those cold and timid souls who know neither victory nor defeat.

THEODORE ROOSEVELT

THE BLACK WIDOW'S GUIDE
TO KILLER POOL

INTRODUCTION

I was twenty-two the first time I entered "the zone." It was like nothing I had ever experienced. Ball after ball went tumbling into the pocket, almost before I knew I had taken a shot.

Stripes and solids, bank shots, cut shots, and combinations. One after another. I lost count pretty quickly, but my mentor, Gene Nagy, kept a tally as he set up each new rack.

We were out in Queens, at a café known as La Cue, where I played every day with Gene. He had the perfect personality for a mentor, and with his long, flowing white beard, he even looked like a guru.

A crowd gathered around us, but I didn't notice. All I saw was the table, as it gradually revealed its mysteries. Somehow, for the first time in my life, I truly could not miss.

When at last it ended, on an impossible lie, I was ecstatic. One hundred and twenty-two balls! I had never heard of a woman topping one hundred, and I thought for sure I had scaled the mountaintop.

Then Gene chalked up. In the very next inning, he started a streak that ran for 230 consecutive shots. He didn't say a word, but I learned plenty just the same.

I learned there is always room for improvement in this game. I'm still learning that, at every tournament and during every practice session. To me, that's what makes pool so incredible—you can't master it, but you can always get better.

See, I wasn't always the Black Widow. I got that nickname from some guys in a local poolroom, because I always wore black and I looked deadly at the table. But when I walked into a poolroom for the first time ten years ago, I was just Jeanette, an eighteen-year-old dropout, a rebel, a waitress trying to make the rent on my studio in Manhattan.

No one could have predicted that I would succeed at pool. I was the wrong sex. I was too old—most of pool's champions started shooting as children. Plus, I had a distinct physical handicap for a sport that requires constant bending: scoliosis. My spine was curved, and I would have been a hunchback were it not for eighteen inches of metal rod implanted in my back.

But five years later, I was ranked as the number one pool player on the face of the earth. Since then, I have helped lead the women's game out of obscurity and into the limelight, made the quickest run from nowhere to number one in the history of the game, and earned more money than any other professional playing today.

I was a scrawny, handicapped girl. Now I'm a champion. I have done motivational speaking for Fortune 500 companies and top-notch universities. In every city on the tour, I see young girls who tell me they want to grow up and be like me. I've got an image as both a dedicated athlete and a sophisticated woman who takes what she wants.

That eighteen-year-old waitress has become a twenty-eight-year-old married woman, a spokeswoman for national charities, and an athlete making mortgage payments on a giant ranch house in the Midwest.

The transformation wasn't easy. I could have quit a thousand times, after bitter losses, close calls, and hospital visits, but I never did, because in my heart I knew I could make it, even though everyone else thought it was unrealistic.

I had to learn all the techniques I will share with you in this book—from how to make a bridge to how to sink a bank shot with a TV camera in your face.

But the lessons I have learned can make you more than just the player to beat in your basement, bar league, or tournament.

I have learned how to compete, how to lose gracefully and win frequently. I have come to understand the psychology of success, the importance of mental toughness. I have learned the difference between competing against men and against women. I know how to stay focused under pressure, and how to achieve goals in the face of seemingly impossible odds. I am learning how to handle success, and how to balance a career and a family.

And now I want to share my secrets.

These secrets can help you succeed, whether or not you ever pick up a cue stick. They were learned in the poolroom, but the mental, analytical, and psychological techniques also work at home and in the office.

I am not vain enough or dumb enough to tell you that you have to do it my way. The point of this book is to give you the courage to find your own way.

I could have written this book a number of ways. I could have whipped off a "rack 'em and crack 'em" paperback, like some other pros have done. Pool hacks told me I could just cut and paste their instructions, slap a sexy photo on the cover, and start collecting royalties.

Publishing houses approached me three years ago with a list of potential co-authors. These writers promised me that we would never have to meet. I could talk for a few hours into a tape recorder, and they would transform these tapes into a "personality" book.

"That's the way it's done," they told me.

Well, that's not how I wanted it done.

I waited until I met Adam Scott Gershenson, who was writing then for the *New York Times*. I saw an article of his about the Women's Professional Billiard Association's Big Apple Classic that captured both the excitement of the sport and the unique role women played in transforming what was once a hustler's game into a family event.

As we got to know each other, it became clear that we both wanted a book that would tell my story and help readers learn to play better pool.

One of the frustrating things about writing a book is that sometimes it feels like sending a message in a bottle. I don't want to wait around on the beach forever without hearing your responses, so please feel free to contact me through my Web site, at www. jeanettelee.com.

Turn the page, and I'll welcome you to my web.

HOW TO PLAY

YOUR TRUE POTENTIAL

I walked into Chelsea Billiards on a spring day in 1989, after *The Color of Money,* starring Tom Cruise and Paul Newman, had come out. In the movie, the girl never takes a shot; she's just an accessory. Still, something about the sight of these two sexy hustlers making their living off playing this game appealed to me.

At that time, Chelsea Billiards was the best room in town. It offered a cross section of society, from uptown millionaires to downtown scam artists, and everybody in between.

But the player who caught my eye was an old man shooting pool by himself, over on the house table reserved for the regulars. Johnny Ervolino. He moved so gracefully around the table, like a dancer or an angel. So calm, so steady. Even from across the room, I could see him drawing long, deep, even breaths. I could see the arteries pulsing in his neck.

Too shy to approach, I stared from a distance. He was an artist, it seemed to me then, a genius with a cue instead of a paintbrush. With every stroke, the patterns changed, scattering and resolving into a new image, a new world, a new puzzle to figure out. And after every shot, if I listened closely enough, I swore that I could hear in the distance the satisfying thud of another ball tumbling into a leather pocket.

When I pulled a cue off the wall, I knew immediately that I lacked his touch, his feel for the game, his knowledge, and his skill. Heck, I didn't even have any idea about how to stand.

I didn't know it at the time, but I was already learning my first lesson: you cannot judge a pool player's potential at a glance.

It seems so easy. You walk into a place, you see two kinds of players. On one table prowls the cool cat, with the smooth, easy stroke and the attitude to match. Two tables over, an obvious hack strains and sweats beneath the lights, with chalk on her hands and a frown on her face.

The cat glides around the table, displaying all the apparent signs of greatness—creativity, concentration, and confidence. The hack is painful to watch. Her arm seems to creak with every stroke.

So there you have it. The first player has a future in pool, while the second ought to get that elbow greased and oiled.

But it's just not that easy.

When I started playing pool, I was definitely a hack. And even though they might not want to admit it, I'm pretty sure the same is true for every other legendary pool player. None of us were born great. It's just not that kind of sport. First you have to learn how to play, and then, more important, how to win.

I wish I could explain how that first day in the poolroom affected me. But how do you explain being struck by lightning? It was that powerful, that sudden a love affair.

I knew right away that I wanted to be the best player that ever lived.

My friends laughed, and with good reason. I was the worst player out of all of us. Meanwhile, my doctors were insisting that I not play, because they knew that the strain would eventually overwhelm the metal rod that runs the length of my spine and keeps me walking upright. And then there was the surest sign that I was no good: the guys in the poolroom lined up to play me for money.

What none of us realized, though, is that true potential lies hidden beneath the surface. The player who is willing to read this book, study the game, practice correctly, and understand the mental and psychological aspects of pool will grow into a far better player than the show-off who relies on his or her natural ability.

I'm not about to name names, but there are plenty of top players on the Women's Professional Billiard Association Tour with little or no natural talent. And believe it or not, they win. They win major tournaments and pull in serious prize money, because they have dedicated themselves to the sport, and they do whatever it takes to get better. Then there are others with tons of natural ability who've yet to cash a winner's check.

That's part of the beauty of pool. So much of the game is mental. You don't have to be seven feet tall or three hundred pounds, and you don't have to run like the wind (unless you've tried to work a hustle that backfired).

Anyone can get very good at pool.

And I have to say thank God for that, because it has changed my life. When I walked into Chelsea Billiards for the first time, I felt like I had nothing going for me.

I had grown up in a family with so little money that when we wanted to hold things together, we used sticky rice instead of Elmer's glue. I wasn't close with my mother or stepfather. My closest relative was my grandmother, only she spoke no English, and I spoke no Korean. My sister was the favorite child, the valedictorian with a future in international business.

I was the runt of the litter, underweight and misunderstood. Bright enough to get into Bronx Science, a magnet school in New York City, but stubborn enough to drop out as soon as I could.

At eighteen, I was a waitress, an aimless party girl who woke up every morning wishing I could be anybody but who I was. I went to a bunch of colleges, but I could never commit myself fully to that kind of education.

Then I discovered pool. And once I did, I was not to be stopped. Looking back, I don't recommend doing what I did. I gave up everything but pool for the next few years, because I believed that was the only way to reach my goal. I am still convinced that you have to sacrifice to become the best player in the world, but I have also learned how important it is to have balance in your life. Believe me, winning your local tournament won't mean as much if you have no one to celebrate with.

Back then, I played more pool than any person should ever be allowed to play. I woke up every morning with a new purpose, determined to make it to the poolroom as quickly as possible. No shower, no makeup, no breakfast.

I lived just three blocks from the hall, but I'd flag a cab anyway, figuring the minutes on the table were worth the money I would spend.

Every day I played fifteen, sixteen hours in a row. Chelsea Billiards never closed, and I rarely left. One time I played thirty-seven hours straight, until my back collapsed and my friends had to carry me home.

Later that week, when I got out of the hospital, I was still obsessed. I would go to cafés and drift off in the middle of conversations, watching imaginary pool balls ricocheting off my friends' heads, against the ceiling, and back down into the garbage can in the corner.

At night, when I lay down to sleep, I would play games in my head. I would shoot my imaginary break and follow the balls as they scattered around the table. Then I would visualize every shot. Even in my imagination, I could not make all of them. In fact, it took me months before I could run a rack, even in my dreams.

I admit, I may have been deranged—but I was happy. For the first time, I had found my passion, found what I was meant to do with my life. I honestly don't think it matters whether your passion is pool or business or building a family or all three—what matters is that you find the strength and the courage and the means to achieve your goal.

You may not want to dedicate your life to pool. Chances are, you just want to beat your father-in-law next Thanksgiving, or your boss at the next corporate event. Part I of this book, which stresses fundamentals and shot making, will teach you the basics of how to play. Maybe you want to dominate the table at the neighborhood pub, or perhaps you're dying to take home the trophy from the local league. Part II, which explores the mental aspects of competition, will teach you how to win and how to play like a professional. No doubt some of you have dreams of joining the pro tour. Part III takes you behind the scenes, so you can see what life is really like on the professional tour.

Of course, you won't get anywhere without a little ambition and a dream. So please, dream big. Because there's one thing I have discovered over the last ten years: people become who they believe they are.

There will be people—there are always people—who will tell you your dreams are not realistic.

But what is realistic? Twenty years ago, if I said you could send messages instantaneously around the world, you might have locked me up. Now it seems like everybody has E-mail. Ten years ago, if I told you that women playing pool in silk and satin would be watched by a million people once a week on ESPN, you would have said I was crazy.

So don't be confined by someone else's version of reality. There is always another side, a hidden, personal side that comes out only when you make it come out. It is your job to transform the reality that everyone else sees into the reality that only you can create.

When I first joined the tour in 1990, people said it wasn't realistic to think that I could beat established top-ranked professionals like Ewa Mataya Laurance and Loree Jon Jones. After all, they had been playing for twenty years. They had more knowledge, more experience, more refined games.

But there was another side to that reality. I knew, each time I went for a shot, that I could make that one shot. And when the next one came up, I could make that one, too.

And so, shot by shot, I managed to make my vision come true. The reality that everyone else saw, the image of a rookie in over her head, didn't really matter anymore. I had created my own universe, in which I was a pool player, making smart decisions, searching for sinkable shots.

Before that year was over, there was a new reality in the tour rankings—I was number one.

So if you're not afraid to dream, and you're willing to work, believe me when I say that anybody can become a champion.

I'm not asking you to play all the time like I did. But I will say this: no matter what you devote yourself to, don't hold back, and don't cheat yourself. Anyone can make excuses, and it is easy to say "I would have been great if only I had tried."

By April 1999, ten years had passed since I'd first seen Johnny Ervolino, the coolest cat in Chelsea Billiards. That's when I saw him again, when the Amsterdam Billiard Club on East Eighty-sixth Street held the 1999 National Straight Pool Championship.

Now, Amsterdam is the top room in the city. I happen to be their in-house professional. And when the straight pool tournament began, I was one of just two women competing against eighty men. The other woman lost in the opening rounds.

I drew Johnny Ervolino. And I beat him.

It was so satisfying. At first, I didn't know why it felt so impor-tant. I had won tournaments all over the world, in front of bigger audiences, and with more money on the line.

But then I realized that it felt so good because I had been trans-formed. I had walked in as the underdog, the know-nothing, the amateur. And walked out, ten years later, as the player to beat.

WHY WE PLAY

If you have found yourself waiting for a table at your local poolroom recently, there's a reason: forty-two million Americans played pool last year. More than football, basketball, or baseball. Nearly twelve million of them played more than twenty-five times, and almost five million people said pool was their favorite activity.

So, why do people love pool so much?

It's hard for me to step back and think about why I love pool so much. It's like asking why I love my mother or my husband. I just do. It stimulates my brain, my body, and my heart.

It helps clear my head, and I think it keeps me sane. It gives me a chance to measure myself every day, to see if I'm getting better, staying the same, or slipping just a little bit.

Most of the time I don't feel like I'm playing well. I could always do better. I think that's why I push myself so hard to improve, because I'm never satisfied. I should have sunk that shot along the rail, should have finished off that last combination. This attitude has made me a better player, but there's a trade-off; sometimes I feel perpetually frustrated.

I wish I could give myself a break, keep in mind the things I'm doing well, instead of the mistakes I'm making. But I can't. And so I become my own slave driver. Whenever I am not ranked number one in the world, I can't stand it—it kills me. I have an incredible will to win and a need to compete.

Thankfully, not everybody plays pool for these reasons.

Almost everyone plays because they have fun doing it. And it's not just because we have fancy billiard rooms now with cappuccino bars and mixed drinks and plenty of chances to meet people while you're waiting for a table. People have been playing pool for over five hundred years on at least three continents, because it is just an amazing game!

There is something about chasing those colored balls around the table that hooks people. Once you catch the bug, you're addicted. Luckily, it's a harmless obsession. You won't neglect your family, and you won't be sticking needles in your veins. You'll just find yourself either playing pool or thinking about it constantly.

And you won't be alone. Pool is one of the most social sports on the planet. You can play pool on a date, or as part of a night on the town. But please, if you are playing pool on a date, promise me one thing: never lose on purpose. If he isn't man enough to accept being beaten by a woman, then he's not good enough for you anyway. Besides, think of the precedent you'd be setting.

I think so many people love pool because it stimulates their brain. Pool forces you to think ahead, to visualize possibilities before they happen. Ninety percent of pool takes place in your mind, and only 10 percent is actually played out on the table. That is why this book will focus so much on the mental aspects of the game.

To me, pool is like chess, only you don't have to worry about losing to a computer. Every moment at the table forces you to think— about strategy and angles, patterns and sequences. You are always looking ahead to the next shot, mapping out alternatives in your brain. You can learn physics, geometry, and, of course, English, on a pool table, as I'll explain later.

Pool is also a lot like golf in that finesse and shot-making ability are ultimately more important than brute force. In fact, aside from driving, putting, and chipping, it's the same game. Pool might also be the most democratic game on earth.

Anyone can play. Even better, anyone can win.

It doesn't matter if you're rich or poor, young or old, big or small, male or female, black, white, or yellow. No one has an innate advantage over anyone else when they come to the pool table. Everyone starts out equal.

You don't need an acre of green grass to play, or even a hundred yards of AstroTurf. You don't even need ninety-four feet of hardwood floor, or a fenced-in asphalt playground. Pool tables come in a variety of sizes, but very few of them are larger than four and a half feet by nine feet.

You can find that space in the ritziest country club and the dirtiest backwater dive. And the best part is that if you took the player from that dive and waltzed him into the country club, he would have a fair shot at beating anyone in the place.

On a professional level, women even have advantages over men. We make twice as much money, when you factor in sponsorship deals, prize money, signature memorabilia, endorsements, and exhibition appearances. Our following dwarfs theirs, because we are constantly on television. That's pretty rare in sports, and especially when you realize that ten years ago, nobody had ever heard of women's pool.

And it's not just because we're cute.

Pool is one of the few sports where women can hold their own against men. There is no hitting, and endurance isn't usually a factor. Strength comes into play on the break shot, but after that, finesse and foresight are the most important elements in successful pool—two traits not commonly associated with the average male.

The table is level, both physically and symbolically. In the early days of pool, only men were allowed to use a cue stick with a tip. Women were forced to use a blunt mace (basically a fat stick with a round end), because men claimed to be afraid that we would rip the cloth. Since the mid–nineteenth century, though, we've been allowed to use the same stick as the men. Now they're not worried about the cloth anymore—they're only afraid they'll be racking too often after we beat them.

They have reason to be afraid. Women have made incredible strides in pool. In 1993, the Women's Professional Billiard Association held its first Classic Tour. That year, we were on television for all of four hours. In 1998, we were on for more than fifty! Pool will be an exhibition sport in the 2002 summer Olympic games, and a medal sport in 2006. If they ever make a third *Hustler* movie, you can bet it'll be about women's pool. Maybe they'll get Tom Cruise to carry my cues from town to town!

Because pool gives everyone an equal shot at greatness, it also provides every player with a chance to define him- or herself.

I think that this, more than anything else, is what makes the game so popular. You might be a giggling girl 99 percent of the time, but when it's time to aim and fire, you can get intensely serious. You might be a shy guy, but you can let your play talk for you. You might be seventy, eighty, ninety years old, but when they rack the balls, you can beat the pants off that little whippersnapper across the table.

The question becomes, Who do you want to be when you step up to the table? You can shed your old identity like a snake growing out of its skin and become the person you have always wanted to be. There are no preconceived notions of how you play based on how you look or talk or act.

I'm not going to ruin all that by telling you you've got to be like me or play like me or dress like me or make those fierce faces I make at the table. You can develop your own persona, your own being, right there while you're playing.

The only thing I want to do is to help you become the best player you can be. Because let's face it: even a great game like pool that challenges your mind, gives everyone a fair shot, and allows you to become the person you've always wanted to be is a heck of a lot more fun when you win.

TOOLS OF THE TRADE

3

TAKE YOUR CUE

The first time I played, I yanked a cue out of the rack on the wall and rolled it on the table. I didn't know why I was doing it, but everyone else was, so I figured it was important.

Later I learned that they were checking for imperfections in the cue—if it wobbled when it rolled, that meant the cue was off-line, or warped.

Later still I learned that there is another way to check for these imperfections. Just hold the cue out straight, close one eye, and look down the length of the cue like a sniper scoping out a rifle.

Last, I learned that it just doesn't matter that much. The imperfections of a house cue may affect your shooting, but as long as they are not glaring, you can overcome them. Just aim carefully and stroke smoothly the way I will teach you to, and you won't have to worry too much about a slight warp in the stick.

Checking the cue for imperfections instead of checking yourself and your game is a clear case of blaming the arrow instead of the archer. But it is the archer who shoots, and the archer who must take the credit—and the blame—for the results on the table. Next time you hear a victorious player (who doesn't have an endorsement contract) give credit for his win to his cue stick, feel free to start blaming your cue for the loss.

I'm not saying you should confine yourself to using a beat-up house cue for the rest of your life. If you are at all serious about pool, you should buy yourself a two-piece custom cue.

If there was no other advantage to owning your own cue, the consistency it provides would be enough. Just as you will learn to make your stance, aim, and grip consistent, you want a consistent cue. View the game as a controlled experiment: the more elements you keep the same, the easier it is to diagnose any flaws in your game when things go badly.

Please, don't tell yourself you're not good enough to own your own cue, and don't listen if anyone laughs at you for buying one. It is both a present to yourself and a commitment to your sport. If they don't want to buy their own cue, fine. That's up to them. If you want to get better, buy a cue. You'll play more often, and you'll soon be beating them, if you're not already. Around that time, they'll start asking you where you bought your cue.

I got my very first custom cue after I had been playing about six months. It wasn't exactly a planned event. It started one afternoon when a very rich man came into Chelsea Billiards. I had seen him around before, flashing his money and his platinum watch.

He wasn't a bad player, but he didn't take me seriously. He asked me to play him for twenty dollars a game, and offered me a ridiculous handicap. We were playing nine-ball, and he had to make the 9-ball to win, but I was spotted the 7-out, which meant that I could win by sinking the 7, 8, or 9. He was the first of many guys to underestimate me.

The truth is, I couldn't really afford to lose. Sure, I had the twenty bucks in my pocket, but I was living on waitress wages at the time. If I lost more than a couple of games, I would have had to give up some of the luxuries in my life—like heat and food.

The games lasted about two minutes each. The pace and the stakes made me feel like I was standing in front of a roulette wheel in Vegas. Lucky for me, I started winning right away. Rack after rack after rack.

Eventually, he called it quits—down twenty games.

Then he opened his wallet, and it was bare. That is truly bad form, and he probably wouldn't have pulled it on another guy.

But he quickly figured out a way to make good: he offered to take me to a retail billiard store, where I could buy myself a cue on his credit card.

I was eighteen years old, and I took my time and seriously considered the most important factor: looks. I took home the prettiest cue in the place, with inlaid designs and a shiny finish, for four hundred dollars.

But just in case you want to buy a cue using more practical considerations, let me tell you what to look for. You can get a good two-piece cue for somewhere between $150 and $400. The prime advantage of a two-piece cue is that it can be broken down and carried easily.

You're paying for the quality of the wood, the name brand, and the workmanship, which ensures that your cue will last for years without warping or cracking.

The first thing to keep in mind is the weight of the cue. No matter what you may have heard, size does matter. House cues generally have their weight in ounces stamped along the shaft. Custom cues typically do not.

I use a 19-ounce cue. Anywhere between $18\frac{1}{2}$ and $19\frac{1}{2}$ ounces is standard. I happen to like the solid feel of a 19-ounce stick in my hands. I used to think that you could determine how heavy your cue should be by your height and weight, but that's just not so.

A cue is like a baseball bat—some players want a lighter stick for greater speed and control, others prefer a heavier stick with more solidity and mass. Neither stick necessarily provides more power, because momentum is determined by both speed and mass, and the heavier the cue, the slower it moves.

Get a cue you feel comfortable with, and don't obsess about the weight. Obsessing about weight is never a good thing. Whatever weight you choose, play with it for at least six months. Develop a feel for the cue. Then, if it feels like it's going to fly out of your hands on every shot, you can have the retail shop put more weight in the bottom of your cue. If the cue feels sluggish and heavy, like you're a lumberjack carrying a log, the professionals at the billiard shop can take some weight out of the bottom.

Listen to yourself when you play. If you never find yourself saying "This cue is too light" or "This cue is too heavy," then you've made the perfect choice.

Pool cues tend to have a uniform length. Even custom cues vary only between 56 and 58 inches, and then only for extremely short or very tall players. I use a 57-inch cue, which works for 99 percent of professional players, regardless of their height. It shouldn't feel like a totem pole in your hand, but it shouldn't feel like a toothpick, either.

The shape of your cue is also a factor to consider. House cues are uniformly tapered from tip to butt. Custom cues typically come with a pro-style taper, which means they maintain a constant diameter from the tip to about 12 inches back, at which point they begin tapering at a constant rate toward the butt of the cue.

My first cue was originally 13 millimeters in diameter. I used so much sandpaper on it, trying to keep it smooth, that I wore it down to $12^3/_4$ millimeters. Then I learned you are never supposed to use sandpaper on your cue; the shops sell shaft paper for that. Shaft paper is designed to keep your cue smooth without sanding it down. Fortuitously, I also learned that I liked the $12^3/_4$-millimeter diameter, and now my custom cues are all this size. Anything in this range should suit you fine.

All these factors can affect your cue's performance, but the most important aspect of your cue is the leather tip. That's the part you're hitting the cue ball with.

Ask for a medium tip. The soft ones lose their shape easily, and they create too much spin. As you improve, move up to a medium-hard tip. When you're putting spin on the ball, as I will explain later, you want it to be intentional, not accidental.

The tip, when seen from the side, should always be half-moon shaped. To make sure that your tip is in the right shape, periodically hold a quarter or a nickel up against it. The shape of the tip should conform to the side of the coin.

If the tip has flattened out, or mushroomed, you can use a tool known as a shaper to hone it again. If it has frayed, your billiard shop will have another tool, called a trimmer; they will also have a scuffer, which is used to keep the tip rough-edged, so that it will catch the chalk when you rub it on the tip before every shot.

The purpose of applying the chalk is to provide friction between the cue tip and the cue ball. This will help you avoid miscues, those embarrassing moments that occur when the cue stick slides harmlessly off the cue ball instead of striking it properly.

If you want your cue to last, never leave it in the trunk of a car, or anyplace else where it gets very hot or very cold. Wood is a breathing material that expands and contracts, as you probably notice when your wooden doors swell in the humidity of summertime and become difficult to close. You don't want your cue swelling and shrinking—the whole reason you bought it was for consistency, remember?

To keep your cue clean, you can buy cue cleaners, or you can burnish it down with a wrapped dollar bill or a business card. The best thing to use, though, is a piece of leather. Some people prefer to just wipe the shaft with a slightly damp cloth. Don't use a sopping wet cloth, and be careful not to wet the grip, which can be made of leather, nylon, or Irish linen. I use Irish linen because it is the most absorbent and it looks the best. I find the nylon wrap to be the worst of the three, but it is the cheapest, and none of the grips will adversely affect your game.

I'm actually not too obsessive about keeping my cue clean. I don't mind a little chalk residue on the shaft—it adds character.

That doesn't mean I don't care for my personal cues. For instance, I would never use a cue as a hook, like some people do, to gather balls from around the table before I rack. I mean, please: get some exercise, walk around the table. You won't have a coronary. Besides, using your cue like that will put serious dings in your shaft. These dings will bother you later when you are shooting, because you'll feel them every time you slide the cue through your bridge hand.

Of course, if you play a lot, eventually you're going to get some dings in your cue, so you should know how to eliminate them. Steam them out. Moisten a Q-Tip, rub it over the dinged area, then press it briefly with a hot iron. That will raise the wood, and you can smooth it out again with the shaft paper.

As you get more serious and more interested in racking up trophies for the empty case in the hall, you may want to buy extra cues. It's one way to add a few more arrows to your quiver.

First, you can buy an extra shaft for your custom cue, so that if anything happens to the tip or the shaft during a tournament, you can pull the spare out of your case, screw it on, and keep playing. I've heard stories of cues splitting, shafts splintering, and butts shattering. If you don't have a backup or a break cue, you might have to use a cue off the house rack, which could frustrate you and disrupt your concentration.

Next you may want a break cue. This is, as you may have guessed, a cue used only for breaking. In nine-ball, the game we play on television, a powerful break can mean the difference between a $60,000 paycheck and a pat on the back and "You'll get 'em next time" from your opponent.

To generate this kind of power, you have to hit the cue ball hard. Doing this with your game cue could damage the tip or crack the ferrule, the white casing below the tip that connects the tip to the shaft.

Some players like a heavier cue for this task; I take a cue with a flatter tip and go half an ounce lighter. That's because I want to generate my power through the speed of my stroke. Either way, do what feels best. Some players get a break cue with identical specifications to their game cue, because they trust how it feels.

A third cue you might want to buy is a jump cue. With rare exceptions, every professional has one, and I will explain its purpose in detail in Chapter 8. For now, know that a jump cue is shorter and lighter than a regular cue, which helps you make the whiplike motion needed to drive the ball down into the slate, so that it bounces up and over the ball blocking your shot. Jump cues are luxury items; you can jump balls with regular cues, but it is harder.

GLOVE LOVE

I wear a glove whenever I shoot pool. Almost no other professional wears a glove, and I don't see why not. A glove provides the essence of consistency, and it saves me from having to put baby powder on my hands to smooth out the friction between the cue and my flesh.

I don't sacrifice any sensitivity, and I never have to worry about the conditions in the room. Whether it's dry, whether it's sticky or clammy, it makes no difference—I've always got a nice, smooth passageway with the glove, which is a combination of nylon and spandex. Gloves come in different sizes and colors, and you can get them at any decent pro shop. Again, don't make your decision based on what other people will say. I promise you, you won't look like a Michael Jackson retread (unless you buy one with sequins).

Today, the glove is part of my trademark look, but it started out as a lark. I had been to a very fancy party on the Upper East Side, where I wore long silk gloves that stretched all the way up my arms.

After the party, we decided to unwind and play some pool. I didn't feel like taking my gloves off, so I started playing with them on. Wow! It felt so smooth. No powder, no friction, no problem.

The next morning, I cut those gloves at the wrist. For the next few months, I always played with one on my bridge hand. Then I spotted one of the male players, a straight pool champion named Danny Barudy, wearing something strange on his hand.

What's that? I asked.

A pool glove, he said.

I hadn't even known they existed, but later that week I went out and bought one. It was even better than my five-fingered glove, because it covered my palm, my thumb, and the two fingers on my bridge hand that touch the cue, but it also left my pinky and ring finger free so I could feel the table beneath my fingertips.

PUTTING IT ON THE TABLE

Buying a pool table is like buying an expensive, permanent piece of furniture for your home. Yet for some reason it is a piece of furniture that men are actually interested in. This may be the most unique feature of a pool table. Have you ever heard of a man bragging that he just bought the most precious divan? Or how the love seat matches the carpet? Unlikely. But he will tell all his friends about the table. And they will all start to come over. And drink your beer, and call you "honey" after a couple of rounds, and you will have to tell your significant other to get his drunken friends out of the house before you brain one of them with the 8-ball.

But that's another issue.

For now, let's go shopping.

Owning your own table is not an essential part of becoming a great pool player, any more than owning your own gym is essential to becoming a bodybuilder.

But it helps.

The convenience of a home table makes it that much easier to practice the skills you'll be learning in this book.

But what should you buy?

Tables come in different sizes. The table we call a bar box is three and a half feet by seven feet. That's the size you will find in

Diagram I
YOUR BASIC TABLE

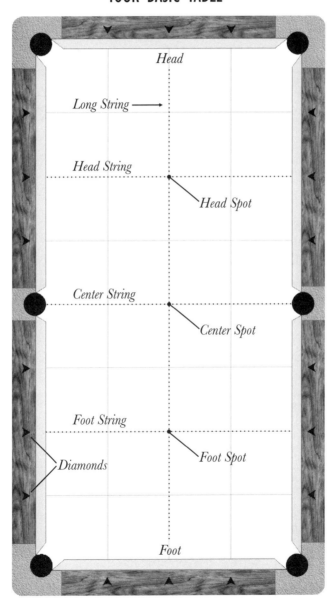

Head

Long String ⟶

Head String

Head Spot

Center String

Center Spot

Foot String

Diamonds

Foot Spot

Foot

most bars, and I think it is a little smaller than the table you'd want for your home.

Four by eight is the standard home-table size, which should fit in most recreation rooms and basements.

Then there's the mother of all pool tables, the four and a half foot by nine foot monster that we use on the professional tour. This is the size I have in my house, and I think it would be stupid for me not to. After you get used to playing on this size table, the bar box feels like a sandbox.

If you can fit a four and a half by nine table in your home, I recommend it. It takes a little more skill, power, and accuracy to pocket balls on a larger table, and it will prepare you better if you one day hope to play in tournament matches.

Remember this, though: don't just take a tape measure, walk off nine feet, and say it fits. You need at least five feet of room on all sides of the table. That is because when the ball is against the close rail, you have to be able to place your bridge hand forward, assume your stance, and take a full backswing. When you do this, the butt of your cue winds up a good five feet from the table. So make sure you have this extra room.

If your room is cursed with one or two unavoidable poles or obstacles, that is surmountable—buy shorty cues. But you don't want to play the whole game like that. It's like playing basketball on your knees.

As for the type of table you buy, that's up to you. Go to your billiard pro shop and ask a lot of questions. The price range is amazing. You can get a good table, with a set of balls and cues, for under $3,000. You can also pay over $100,000 for an antique or custom-designed table.

Ask yourself, though: if you were learning the violin, would you buy a used one from the Salvation Army, a nice, midpriced one, or a top-of-the-line Stradivarius?

It all depends on how much money you have, and how devoted you are to the game. But remember that it doesn't have to cost a fortune.

When you look for a table, you want an elegant piece of furniture that will also provide hours of entertainment for your family. I sponsor and recommend Imperial International, because they're the largest distributor of billiards equipment in the world. They can provide you with everything from the table and cloth to the cues, balls, and chalk. They even have a top-of-the-line Black Widow table, with an all-black finish.

So much of buying a table comes down to personal taste. Maple or oak? Stained or natural? Indoor or out? Do you want drop pockets, where the balls sit after you make them, or an automatic ball-return system?

Some considerations, however, are absolute. When purchasing a table, you are looking for dependability. The rubber cushions should be vibrant and securely attached to the rails. The best tables have artemis rubber.

The slate bed of the table should be perfectly even, and it almost always is. A lot of people buy a table, play for a while, notice the balls rolling in funny directions or at awkward speeds, and decide that their table is a piece of junk. Make sure that the people who install your table use a level to check the table. This problem is more prevalent with tables placed on carpet, because they tend to settle unevenly.

If a problem develops, the table is probably not sitting level. Call the company who delivered and installed the table. They will come out and check it with a level, then adjust the table. Some tables have legs that screw out and extend, but in most cases they will put a shim underneath one or two legs.

Don't try to do this yourself with a matchbook or a packet of sugar like they do at the local diner when your table wobbles. First of all, the table weighs a thousand pounds, so your back might snap. If it doesn't, the slate just might. Wait for the professionals.

Cloths now come in many different colors. I like the classic green, but it doesn't matter much, as long as you can see the balls clearly against the cloth. You don't want to strain your eyes, or you'll take the fun out of playing. Darker colors are preferable to lighter, and studies have shown that green cloths are the easiest on your eyes.

The type of cloth you buy will affect the games played on your table. Some beginners buy a napped cloth. It is less expensive, but it is also coarse, which makes the table slower and tougher to dust and wash. You wind up pushing the balls around as if you were playing shuffleboard.

I prefer a worsted cloth. Although it is more costly, it lasts twice as long. It is also far smoother, sleeker, and faster. On worsted cloth, the game isn't as much about power as it is about finesse, creativity, and touch.

Still, buy what suits your personal needs. When I first started playing basketball, I didn't buy Air Jordans. You can always upgrade your cloth at a later date, although it will cost you a couple hundred dollars. Depending on how often you use the table, you should re-cover it anyway every couple of years—it looks better, and it will play like new again.

Chalk should come with your table. I like blue Master's chalk. It's not too gritty, and it stays on the tip of my cue. That gives me the confidence to stroke any shot without worrying about a potential miscue. That's really what the chalk is all about—keeping your cue stick from sliding off the cue ball at the moment of truth. It's like an antilubricant.

You will also get a set of balls when you buy your table. I recommend Super Pro Aramith Belgian balls. They're not cheap, but they don't flake, chip, or crack like some other balls. Your grandchildren will still be playing with them twenty years after you're gone. If you don't want to go all out, any Belgian balls will do. They are all made well, with vibrant colors and lasting shine. To keep your billiard balls looking good, you can get ball cleaner. You can also simply rinse them occasionally with mild soap and water or wipe them with rubbing alcohol.

To care for your table, buy a brush at any billiard store. Brush the cloth in one direction from head to foot, just as you would brush a thoroughbred horse. Don't forget to brush underneath the rails, just as you would clean behind the ears. Another solution: get a Dustbuster and run it over the cloth now and again to clean up the dust and chalk that accumulates.

Once the table is thoroughly combed and vacuumed, take a barely damp cloth and wipe in the same direction you brushed to lift the dirt off the table. Do not soak the table!

Now that you've got your table all ready, rack 'em up, I'm coming over.

4 FUNDAMENTALS

No matter how much pool you've played, don't skip this chapter. Fundamentals are the key to greatness, and even top professionals have to review them once in a while to make sure that their skills haven't slipped.

A strong base in fundamentals is one aspect of my game that I am very proud of, and it is the one that has never betrayed me in tight situations.

It's the same story in other sports. Michael Jordan was a great basketball player, and everyone ooohed and aahed when he flew through the air to power home a dunk.

But almost everyone in the N.B.A. can dunk.

What set Michael apart and made him a champion was not just above-the-rim acrobatics and prolific scoring. He was incredibly tough mentally and totally sound fundamentally. Think about the last image we are left with from his career. It's the final shot, the jumper to win the championship against Utah, and he executes it perfectly, with the same follow-through every high school coach tries to instill in his players.

Pool is the same way: if you want to succeed on the highest levels, you have got to first understand the fundamentals. They are the foundation of your game, the bedrock upon which everything else rests.

THE GRIP

An old hustler taught me that to properly grip a cue stick, you have to hold it like a baby bird. Not so loose that he'll fly away, but not so tight that you crush him either.

It's good advice. A lot of people don't think much about their grip hand, the one located toward the back of the cue stick. They're too mesmerized by the bridge hand, the one near the cue ball, to pay much attention to their grip.

But there's a reason why players use their dominant hand to grip the back of the cue—right-handers use their right, lefties their left. This hand provides the power, the speed, and the accuracy that I will describe in more detail when it's time to discuss the all-important stroke.

So grab the front of the cue any old way for now, and concentrate on the grip.

Take your dominant arm and swing it all the way back behind you. Then let your elbow drop straight down, as if it were hanging on a hinge. Shake out your hand and wiggle your fingers to loosen them up. You're not shaking hands with your girlfriend's father here, so a strong grip won't do you any good.

Just relax your hand and cradle the stick. Some people stick their pinky out like Queen Elizabeth at teatime, but that's a waste of your energy.

When I cradle the cue in this position, it rests almost completely on my middle finger, and just gently lies across the others. My thumb points toward the ground. Your exact configuration will depend on the shape of your hand and on what feels best for you. The important thing is to be comfortable.

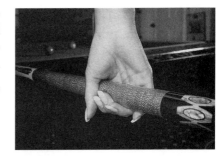

You'll know you are holding the cue too tight if, when you swing, you knock out the lights above your table and cover yourself and your partners in fluorescent shrapnel. Everyone else in the room will also know that you are holding your cue too tight.

As for *where* you should grip the cue, allow form to follow function. Set your front (bridge) hand on the cue stick six to eight inches away from the cue ball. Now start bringing the cue back and forth, as if you were taking practice strokes in anticipation of striking the ball. When the cue stick is just about to make contact with the cue ball, your back arm should be bent at exactly ninety degrees from the elbow. If it is not, move your grip forward or back along the cue stick until you find this point.

You now know everything there is to know about gripping a cue stick.

THE STANCE

There are as many pool stances as there are baseball stances. Mark McGwire doesn't stand like Sammy Sosa, and neither of them stands like Mickey Mantle or Babe Ruth did. So which one's right?

The right stance is the one that feels right for you.

Your body will determine what is comfortable. That doesn't mean you should be shooting pool while doing a flamingo impersonation. The stance must meet three basic needs: it should give you balance, stability, and comfort.

The truth is, I never thought much about my stance, never broke it down or analyzed it. I just got down and played pool. I probably picked it up by osmosis in those first months when I lived at the poolroom and studied every move the best players made.

You should feel free to customize your stance. First, though, I suggest that you should try out the basic elements that make up the conventional player's stance. If it works for you, great. If it doesn't, find your own way. It's like Picasso—he developed his own abstract

style, but first he learned the rigors of realistic drawing. You should know the basics, so that when you do your own thing, you've made your decision from knowledge, not ignorance.

To learn the traditional stance, you first have to figure out how far you should be standing from the table. This distance fluctuates constantly, depending on how far the cue ball is from the rail. You want your bridge hand to rest somewhere between six and eight inches from the cue ball. Any less and your stroke will be choppy; any more and you will lose control of the cue.

Let the situation dictate your distance. If you have to reach halfway over the table to make contact with the cue ball, obviously you do not want to stand three feet away from the table. On the other hand, if the cue ball is lying against the near rail, you are not going to want to stand two inches from the table. Just as you determined where to grip the cue by examining the position of your arm, determine your distance by the position of the cue ball.

Once you've settled on a comfortable distance, it's time to get into the stance. It may not be comfortable right away. It may feel like your first three-piece suit, boring and confining all at once. Relax—you are just trying it on for size.

Set your body so you are fully facing the shot in front of you. Keep your back leg straight, with your toes pointed at a forty-five-degree angle away from the shot.

Now take a step forward and bend your front leg. You want your weight evenly balanced, neither leaning forward nor resting excessively on your back leg.

In this position, you are like a rider on the New York City subway system at rush hour. Imagine people all around you, sweaty, angry, and smelly. You don't want to bump into any of them. But the train is hurtling through the underground and jerking back and forth at high speeds. How do you stay stable? Spread your legs. That way, no matter what direction you are pushed, you will remain upright.

Now bend forward at the waist over the table to start shooting. Really get down on your shot, like a sniper looking down the barrel of a rifle. If your head and shoulders are up, you can't truly commit to the shot. We all have trouble with commitment sometimes, but work on it. Get down and stay down, until you've made your shot and the ball is resting in the pocket.

BRIDGES: A POOL PLAYER'S SUPPORT SYSTEM

But what about that other hand, the bridge hand?

That's the hand that first captivated me that afternoon at Chelsea. What was Johnny Ervolino doing with his fingers, and how was I ever going to learn it?

Don't laugh. I snuck up to his table and watched closely. I was a shameless voyeur, and I recommend that you become one, too. Whenever you see a great player around you, don't be afraid to watch what they're doing. Then later, imitate it yourself. If it works for you and it feels right, incorporate it into your game. If it doesn't, drop it. You don't want to acquire bad habits, but you can always learn something by copying another player's strengths.

I went to extreme lengths to copy Johnny Ervolino's bridge. After studying it for hours, I walked home to my studio apartment, trying to keep my fingers locked into the shape that I saw him using.

But as bedtime approached, I became convinced that I would lose it overnight. And that scared me. I have to say, I had never been so worried about forgetting anything in my life—not my homework, not a cute guy's phone number, nothing.

So I rummaged through my drawers and found a roll of electrical tape. Yes, it's true—in one week, Johnny Ervolino introduced me to both voyeurism and bondage! I wrapped the tape around my left hand, which I had kept frozen in the bridge position. It is no easy thing to wrap your hand in that position. I went between my thumb and fingers and up and around again and again, just to be sure it would hold. And of course every time I relaxed my hand even slightly, it loosened, and I had to add more tape.

I drifted off to sleep like that, and when I woke in the morning, there was my bridge. I padded over to the shower, but once I turned the water on, the tape got wet. As I lathered up the shampoo, the whole sticky mess turned inside out and caught in my hair, and I had to pull it out, piece by piece.

I toweled off and taped my hand up again. So it went for about three weeks. Every time the tape came off, I rigged it up again. When I had no tape, I would just put my fingers in that position and try to keep them there. After about three weeks, I had a sturdy, reliable bridge.

Now, I'm not about to send you running for the electrical tape. I'll explain the two main types of bridges clearly, and I'll also describe some easy ways to remember the alternative bridges, so you won't find yourself cursing me in the shower tomorrow morning.

The Easy Way Across: The Open Bridge

The simplest bridge is known as the open bridge, or V-bridge. It looks very basic, but it is hardly just for beginners. I use this bridge often, because it provides a clearer sight line down the length of the cue and onto the table than the more popular closed bridge.

To make the open or V-bridge, bend over the table, stretch out your arm, and place your hand flat on the table. Then raise your knuckles slightly, but keep your fingertips and the heel of your hand on the table. Slide your thumb up against your forefinger. It will naturally curve upward, creating a V between your thumb and forefinger. That's where the cue goes.

To understand why this is such a helpful bridge, bend down as if you were going to take a shot. Now look down the length of your cue. You can see your shot clearly, like a sniper staring through a scope. This is the bridge you want to use whenever you are hitting the cue ball softly, and when precise aiming is paramount.

Unfortunately, this bridge won't take you everywhere you need to go.

Alternate Route: The Closed Bridge

The closed bridge, which looks complicated but can easily be mastered (with or without electrical tape), is an essential part of every player's arsenal.

The closed bridge is necessary, because when players have to shoot forcefully, the pendulumlike swing naturally brings the cue stick up at the end of a stroke. The closed bridge helps keep the cue level, which keeps you from missing and also keeps the cue from poking out the eye of an innocent bystander walking by your table.

To form the closed bridge, first make a fist with your thumb out and your knuckles down on the table. Spread your pinky, ring, and middle fingers, but leave the thumb and forefinger touching, in their original position.

Put your forefinger tip and thumb tip together, forming a loop. This loop should be touching your middle finger knuckle. Slide the cue stick through the loop, and you're ready for business. The cue should rest primarily on the middle finger.

Now get down again, as if you were taking a shot. You will see that it is slightly more difficult to aim using this bridge, because you cannot see the balls as clearly. Still, you can see over this bridge, and you should grow comfortable with it, especially for break shots or for other times when you need powerful strokes.

Don't forget, when using the closed bridge, that it's called a bridge because it supports your shot. The cue should rest on it. The top finger is simply to keep the cue from rising up into the sky.

Too many players transform the bridge into a kind of wrench, where the top finger controls the cue's movement. This is an easy mistake to make, but it is a fatal one. It will make it nearly impossible for you to develop the smooth, easy stroke that I will describe in the next chapter.

Impassable Roads: The Need for Specialty Bridges

Often, in the course of the game, you will find yourself in a position where you cannot use either the open or the closed bridge. This will happen more frequently when you are facing an advanced player who is purposely leaving you with difficult shots.

Don't panic. *There are ways around every obstacle.*

Let's say you are faced with a shot where you cannot even

hit the cue ball, because another ball is directly in front of it. This situation calls for the elevated bridge. Just make your regular V-bridge, then bring up your wrist. This bridge can feel a little shaky, so try to raise your thumb up as far as you can to stabilize the cue.

Focus on your shot. Don't assume that because you are using an unorthodox bridge you are going to miss the shot. That's self-

▲ Elevated bridge

▲ Open rail bridge
▼ Closed rail bridge

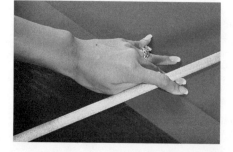

defeating, and it thwarts your growth as a player. Instead, try just a little bit harder, because you know your opponent will be deflated when you sink it.

Now that you've shown you are master of the elevated bridge, your opponent may test you by leaving the cue ball close to the rail. When the cue ball is by the rail, there is no place for you to put down a traditional bridge, so you have to adapt and use a rail bridge.

To make an open rail bridge, form a V-bridge, but this time place your fingers on the wooden rail that runs along the edge of the table. I don't recommend using the closed bridge in this case, because it will raise your cue stick too high—you're already going to hit the cue ball above center, simply because of the height of the rail.

So rest your bridge hand flat on the rail. Now you can guide the cue and keep it straight by using the length of your forefinger and your thumb. Smooth sailing.

If the ball is an inch or so away from the wall, but still too close to lay your bridge hand on the table, use a closed rail bridge.

Lay your hand flat on the rail, and lift your first finger up. Slide your thumb over till your thumb-tip touches your middle knuckle. Rest the shaft on the rail and let these fingers form a wall to guide your stroke. Bring your index finger down and let the cue glide through.

The right way ▲
The wrong way ▼

These rail bridges are helpful on shots where the cue ball is too close. But what if it is too far away? What if you can't reach it and still keep one foot on the floor, which is a basic rule for all pool games?

That's the time to use the mechanical bridge. The mechanical bridge (often called simply "the bridge") is a long cue stick with a grooved metal or plastic extension on the end. You can

typically find the mechanical bridge hanging beneath one side of the pool table. You can use it to support your cue stick in one of several grooves while you aim, just like a bridge you would make with your hand.

Using the mechanical bridge does require some patience, and it looks awkward. For these reasons, it is seldom used, and many players never learn the proper technique for the mechanical bridge. Notice how in the top photo on the preceding page my elbow stays out to the side and doesn't fall down under the cue like in the photo on the bottom. This ensures that my stroke will be level.

But if you can use the bridge effectively, it will open up your game considerably, so it is worth learning the few simple techniques required to master this clumsy-looking skill.

Assuming you are right-handed, hold the bridge in your left hand. Rest it on the table, and line it up in front of the cue ball, facing the direction you want to shoot.

Now, slide the back end over to the left one foot, and put it down. This is the step most players leave out. They try to hold the mechanical bridge in the air in one hand while holding the cue stick in the other hand, and they wind up with no control over either.

So put down the bridge, and hold it down with your left hand.

And forget about it. Literally. It no longer exists, as far as your shot is concerned. The only reason your hand is touching it at all is so you can jerk it up off the table *after* you shoot, in case a ball is coming toward it quickly. Knowing that it will not interfere should give you the peace of mind to focus on, and sink, the shot in front of you.

Use your right hand to lay your cue in one of the grooves. There are several grooves for typical shots, as well as one groove on the side, which you can use if you need an elevated mechanical bridge shot.

Grip your cue right near the butt end. Some people try to shoot these shots overhand, like a baseball pitcher, but that will make your stroke seesaw up and down. What you want to do is turn your elbow up and out, almost parallel to the table. Now when you stroke, the cue will stay level as it slides forward and back. A level stroke translates into more control of the cue ball, which is as important as anything else in the game of pool.

If anyone questions your manhood (or womanhood) when you pull out the bridge, or if they refer to it as "the crutch," or "the ladies' aid," don't listen. There is no reason to be embarrassed when you use the bridge, especially if you can use it to sink your shot. Remember, the truth is, regulation tables are four and a half by nine feet, so even Shaquille O'Neal would need a mechanical bridge every once in a while.

5 THE STROKE

I cannot overemphasize the importance of a smooth, level stroke.

It is, simply, the single most important element in your game. It's the equivalent of a solid swing in golf, tennis, and baseball. That's why, when a player gets hot, they say she's "in stroke" or "in dead stroke."

No one says "Wow, she's dead gripping," or "she's in stance."

Fortunately, it is fairly simple to develop an effective stroke. Just remember that there are three parts to every stroke: backswing, acceleration, and follow-through.

Some professional players use a wide variety of strokes, depending on the result they are looking for on each shot. You may see them use a quick punchy stroke and then, on the next shot, a long fluid stroke. This is like a golfer's mentality applied to pool: you've got your wedge, your driver, and your putter, and you hit differently with each one.

To me, though, consistency is the most important thing. You want to develop one steady stroke that you know will be there for you throughout any match. Even if you do eventually decide to develop multiple strokes, they will all have these things in common: you will always keep your head still, follow through, stay down until the ball is in the pocket, and make sure that you allow your stroke full extension.

To start, you first have to find your solid, comfortable stance and grip the cue with your rear hand. Remember to choose your grip

point by making sure that your lower arm is perpendicular to the ground just before you strike the cue ball.

Now you are ready to start stroking.

COCKING THE GUN: THE BACKSWING

Get into your stance with your rear arm pulled back. With your elbow in the air, let your hand hang straight down loosely, as if your elbow were a well-greased hinge. You will be swinging this lower half of your arm like a pendulum, forward and back. Picture a golf swing, where the backswing just sets up the natural acceleration of the swing.

Remember, your bridge is approximately six to eight inches from the cue ball, and your grip hand will be pointed straight down when your cue touches the cue ball.

As you bend down and prepare to shoot, don't pull your arm back so far that you're straining the shoulder. You don't want any excess tension in your body as you prepare to stroke. This sport is hard enough without bunching up your nerves and tendons. So stay loose. Shake out your hands and fingers and forearm if you have to.

Tightness can lead to tentative, jerky strokes that leave you with no fluidity, and no control over your shot making. That is why some players believe they play better after a drink or two. It relaxes them, and their stroke becomes more fluid. Unfortunately, their concentration also blurs, and when they keep drinking, their vision falters, their breath begins to stink, and they start mumbling incoherent and ineffective pickup lines.

But back to the pendulum swing. Try it first without a cue in hand. Just pull your arm back and let your lower arm dangle loosely from your elbow. This is the stroke you should always use.

Now pick up the cue and try the same motion. If you grip the cue too tightly, you will deprive yourself of this natural movement, so remember not to crush the birdie.

Everyone insists that a level swing is essential, and it is. Nevertheless, the cue will rise slightly on your backswing. Don't worry about it. To keep it perfectly level you would have to contort your arm and shoulder in unimaginably painful ways, and this is simply not necessary. Just make sure you're not sawing at the ball; you should be swinging free and easy, like a pendulum moving back and forth on its own power.

To do this, you have to allow the stroke to accelerate naturally. Your backswing will provide the energy. On the backswing, go from the center position, with your grip hand at a ninety-degree angle from your elbow, and bring it back as far as it will naturally go.

When you want to hit the cue ball hard, bring your arm back a little farther than usual. For gentler "touch" shots, keep the stroke a little "quieter," or shorter.

A warning: you never have to bring your hand all the way back so that your shoulder, elbow, and hand are all in a line. Even on a break shot, where you are looking to generate near-nuclear power, this is overkill.

THE ACCELERATION

From the height of the backswing till the moment your cue connects with the cue ball is, believe it or not, the easy part.

If you've developed a steady bridge and executed a proper backswing, this portion of the stroke comes naturally. Just let your arm fall forward on its hinge.

Still, you cannot lose control during this part of the stroke and

still hope to make a shot. For that reason, it is absolutely essential that you execute practice strokes on every shot, before actually hitting the cue ball.

On these practice strokes, stroke the cue just as close as you can to the cue ball without actually touching it. That way, you will know exactly where you will hit the cue ball. If you stop your practice strokes before this point, you will know only what is going to happen through a portion of your real stroke, not the whole thing. You are leaving the remaining portion to chance, which can only hurt you.

Properly executed practice strokes let you feel your stroke; they also allow you to see if you will hit the cue ball *exactly* where you want to. As I will explain in Chapter 7, where you hit the cue ball will determine whether you sink the ball you're aiming for, as well as where your cue ball will wind up for your next shot.

So take these practice strokes and get comfortable. Let the cue come right up to where it almost touches the cue ball.

On the final stroke, keep the cue as straight and level as possible and stroke from your elbow, not your shoulder. If you've been true to your backswing, the contact with the cue ball will feel right; then you simply have to allow yourself to follow through.

THE FOLLOW-THROUGH

Follow-through is a mystery. It shouldn't matter, but it does. Big time. A stroke that stops just after contact with the cue ball is invariably short, jerky, and ineffective.

It makes no sense, of course: the ball has already been struck— what difference could your actions make after that point? Nevertheless, I know that follow-through does make a noticeable difference. Imagine a baseball player who took a mighty cut and stopped as soon as the bat made contact with the ball. Or a tennis player whose racket froze in midstroke. It doesn't happen, because following through helps keep the rest of the stroke in line.

In pool, you should follow through at least twelve to eighteen inches on every shot. Sometimes the lay of the table makes this impossible—you are not allowed to strike balls other than the cue ball, and you cannot touch any ball while the shot is in progress. Yet whenever possible, try to shoot through the cue ball by this distance.

If you don't, your stroke will become jerky, and your accuracy will disappear. So remember: all the way back, all the way through.

It's an easy mantra, something you can meditate on, or repeat a few times before you go to bed at night.

People have always told me that I have a long stroke. The insinuation, of course, is that it's too long. Maybe. All I know is that it has served me well, and I like it. Earl Strickland and Efren Reyes, two of the greatest male players of all time, also have long strokes, and I haven't seen it doing them any harm.

Perhaps it is easier to control a shorter stroke, but the important thing is to find a stroke you can live with. In truth, everything else is extra. If you don't develop a reliable stroke, you will severely cramp your ability to grow as a player.

Still, finding your stroke doesn't take years of practice. When I started out, I was so determined to master my stroke that I would practice with an imaginary cue stick while riding the subway in Manhattan. I drew quite a few stares, but after a couple of months I'd developed a stroke I could trust.

SOFT STROKES

Almost any woman will tell you: soft strokes are better.

In pool, there are only two kinds of stroke you need—soft and softer.

Beginners tend to bang balls around as if they don't believe they have the power to send a round ball across a flat surface.

This is not baseball, where the bleachers are four hundred feet away; our tables are only nine feet long.

To get an idea of how softly you should hit a ball, do what we call a lag. This is the way that professionals determine who breaks: each player strikes a cue ball. The ball hits the rail at the foot of the table and returns. The player whose shot winds up nearest the rail at the head of the table then decides who breaks. In most games, you will want to break, but in straight pool, it is actually a disadvantage, as I will explain in Chapter 10.

When you lag, be sure to notice how little effort it takes to send the cue ball the length of the table—twice. In game situations, you will almost never need to take a shot that requires you to send a ball careening across three rails. If you do, look for another shot.

With that in mind, the lag will tell you the speed of the table you're playing on, which should help you gauge how hard to hit your shots for the rest of the day or night. It is not a matter of computing exact distances, but rather of developing a feel for the table, a sense that an easy stroke will move the balls far enough.

If you're not convinced, line up a shot a foot away from the side pocket. Put the cue ball straight on, so it is a simple shot. Now try to hit the object ball so that it goes in the direction of the pocket but does not make it all the way there. It's hard. The truth is, the ball wants to keep rolling to the pocket. Let it. Why try to force something that is going to happen naturally anyway?

In time, you will develop a feel, a sense of how each table plays, and exactly how hard you will have to hit the cue ball. Except for the break shot, if you're going to err, always choose to err on the side of hitting too lightly. We know you've got the power to send the cue ball flying, but in pool, power is not as valuable as control.

6 TAKE AIM

Aiming is very difficult to explain in words, and very simple to understand intuitively. The basic idea is that you figure out, on each shot, where the cue ball has to hit the object ball in order to pocket that ball.

Easy.

The only problem, though, is that the point you actually aim for is almost never the point where the balls make contact. That's because the balls are spheres, and it is their edges, not their centers, that touch.

THE CUT SHOT

On shots that are exactly straight on, your aiming point and contact point are the same. Don't celebrate just yet, though. You are almost never faced with a perfect straight-on shot. If all pool shots were straight-on, it would be a very easy and very boring pastime, instead of the frustrating, challenging sport that it is.

So get used to it. Anytime you don't have a straight-on shot, your angle of approach changes. The more severe your angle, the greater the discrepancy will be between your aiming point and your contact point.

We call these angled shots cut shots, and those shots where the cue just skims the object ball we call thin cuts. The thinner the cut, the more your contact point differs from your aiming point.

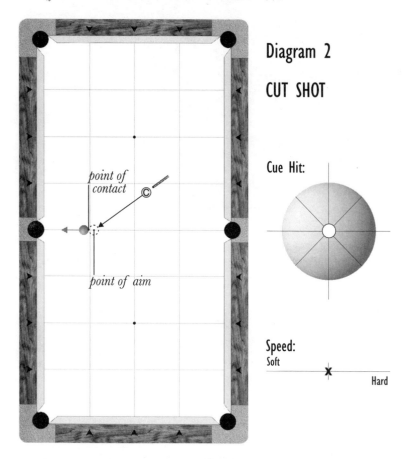

Diagram 2

CUT SHOT

point of
contact

point of aim

Cue Hit:

Speed:
Soft

Hard

Diagram 2 shows why the thinnest shots are the most difficult. You aim for the spot that you think is right, but the cue ball hits the object ball in a different place, and the result is a miss.

There is a system designed to help players overcome this very problem. It's called the ghost-ball system of aiming. The ghost-ball system requires a little imagination to work, the way most ghost stories do. When using the ghost-ball system, the first thing you must do is draw an imaginary line from the pocket you are aiming at through the center of the object ball. Let this imaginary line continue to the far edge of the object ball, where the cue ball will, hopefully, make contact.

Now visualize the cue ball up against the contact point that you just established. Picture the exact center of that ghost cue ball. With the placement firmly entrenched in your mind, aim the cue ball to fill the place of the ghost ball, as shown in Diagram 3, so that it winds up exactly where the ghost ball sits. Your object ball should be spooked enough to head straight for the pocket.

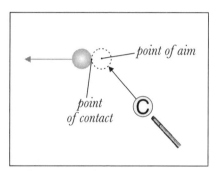

point of aim

point of contact

Diagram 3

GHOST-BALL SYSTEM OF AIMING

This system works well for a lot of players. The thing is, I don't believe in ghosts. I think that if there were a perfect system for aiming, no one would ever miss. And it doesn't matter if you're a beginner or a world champion, you're going to miss sometimes.

So this is my decidedly unglamorous advice: shoot shots. Get a basic idea of what it's going to take to make a specific shot. If you're wrong, don't just curse and kick the table. Remember what you did. Then adjust. The only way to sharpen your aim is to shoot thousands of balls, over and over again, until it becomes second nature.

Sorry.

I talked about this with my friend Reggie Miller, the All-Star shooting guard for the Indiana Pacers. Reggie told me there is only one system that teaches you how to knock down a jump shot—your central nervous system. It takes time to coordinate your eyes and hands, and you have to make constant adjustments.

Don't be afraid to try the ghost-ball system—it might work better for you than it does for me. Still, there is no substitute for focused practice time when it comes to improving your aim.

As you improve, be sure that you focus on one specific point on

the object ball. For you to improve your accuracy, this aiming point should be the smallest target possible. It sounds basic, but it is easy to forget—many times after I miss, I'll realize that I was aiming for a general area on the object ball instead of a precise target point. That's sloppy, and the results are predictable.

Precision is the key.

With that understood, you can relax a little bit. You don't necessarily have to hit that point right on the dot. Pockets are wide and forgiving. Two pool balls can fit, side by side, in the mouth of a pocket. So you don't have to send the ball into the dead center of the pocket. In fact, it's often better to aim for the edge of the pocket, which will guide the ball home, provided you use a gentle stroke.

One final point. Before you shoot, your eyes should flit back and forth from the cue ball to the object ball, as if creating a visual thread between them. Then, when you've finished your practice strokes and are ready to pull the trigger, don't look at the cue ball. Focus solely on the object ball. Your stroke is fine; you've lined it up with the practice strokes. Now is the time to laser in on the aiming point, and let your body do the rest.

Taking my eye off the object ball has cost me more tournaments than I care to think about. Don't let it happen to you.

TAKING CONTROL

The object of pool is not to make shots.

The object of pool is to make shots *and* set up your following shot.

So far, you've learned how to accomplish the first part. Using a stable stance, a comfortable grip, a sturdy bridge, a level stroke, and an accurate aim, you can sink the 5-ball in the corner whenever you want.

Unfortunately, if you are playing nine-ball, you then have to make the 6, or relinquish the table to your opponent.

Yet you cannot just shoot, see that you made your shot, then look up and try to figure out your next move. Long runs of sinking balls do not happen by accident. You have to plan ahead and design your shot so that you not only sink the ball but also leave yourself another makable shot.

To do that, you need to understand some basic principles of cue-ball control.

You may have noticed, while practicing your stroke and refining your aim, that when the cue ball hits an object ball, it rebounds at a ninety-degree angle. That is the natural result of a good solid stroke, in which you strike the cue ball dead-center.

This dead-center stroke is the most important one to master. There are times, however, when you do not want the cue ball to go bounding off at a ninety-degree angle. You may want the cue ball to stop right after it hits the object ball, in order to line up your next shot. Or you may need the cue ball to follow the object ball—not all the way into the pocket, but a little ways down the table. There are also times when you want the cue ball to come back to you after colliding with the object ball, the way a yo-yo returns to its owner after it reaches the end of its string.

There are ways to achieve all of these goals. While recreational players may never realize these essential tools of the trade, a player who studies the game and is looking to improve will be lost without them.

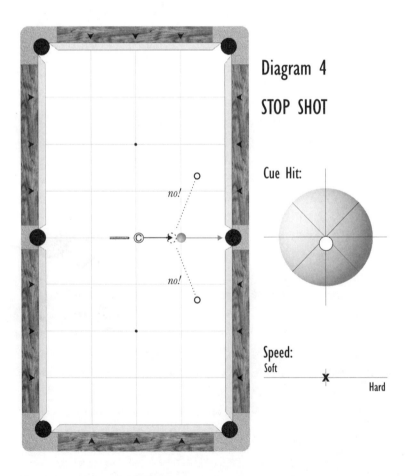

Diagram 4
STOP SHOT

no!

no!

Cue Hit:

Speed:
Soft

Hard

RED LIGHT: THE STOP SHOT

To make the cue ball stop where it hits the object ball on a straight shot, strike the cue ball immediately below center, with the force of a medium hit, as shown in Diagram 4. If you aim correctly, the cue ball should strike the object ball, sending the ball scurrying to its pocket, and stop dead in its tracks.

Practice this shot at different speeds, and try it when the object ball is far from the cue ball. The farther away the object ball is, the harder you have to hit it; you also have to hit slightly lower on the cue ball to make it stop where you want it to.

Don't go too low on the stop shot, or you will wind up causing the ball to come back to you, like an old boyfriend calling at two in the morning. You don't want to encourage this kind of behavior.

FOLLOW THE LEADER: THE FOLLOW SHOT

Sometimes you need the cue ball to keep going in the same direction as the object ball after contact. This is an easy effect to achieve. What you want to do is to hit the cue ball about half an inch above its center. Luckily, the diameter of your cue stick's tip is roughly half an inch; so picture hitting the ball one cue tip above center.

The results are shown in Diagram 5. Strike the cue ball using a medium-speed stroke, stay down, follow through, and let the weight of the cue do the work for you.

On a straight-on shot, it would be easy to scratch using this stroke. If you are in danger of pocketing the cue ball, strike the follow shot very gently, or hit it at an angle, so that it cuts the object ball instead of hitting it straight on and following directly in its path.

If you want the cue ball to follow the object ball for only a couple of inches after contact, use the center ball follow shot shown in Diagram 6. The ball will slide forward slightly after contact with the object ball, but it will not roll.

For both types of follow shots, remember to keep your stroke level. This may sound paradoxical, keeping the cue level while striking the ball higher, but it is not. To compensate, pull the fingers on your bridge hand closer together, and elevate the bridge. That way, you strike the ball where you want to, without sacrificing the level stroke it took so long to master.

Remember too, the farther away from center you hit the cue ball, the more important it is to chalk up. It is much easier to miscue, because you have less margin for error when you are not striking the cue ball dead-on.

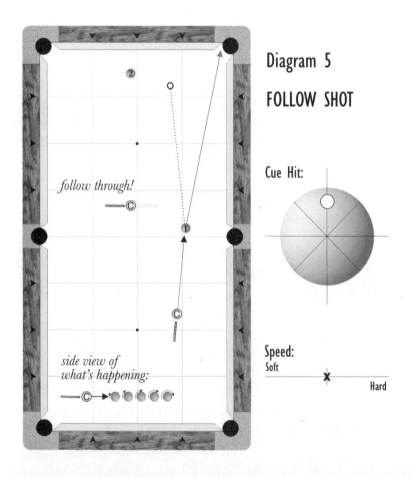

Diagram 5

FOLLOW SHOT

follow through!

side view of what's happening:

Cue Hit:

Speed:
Soft

Hard

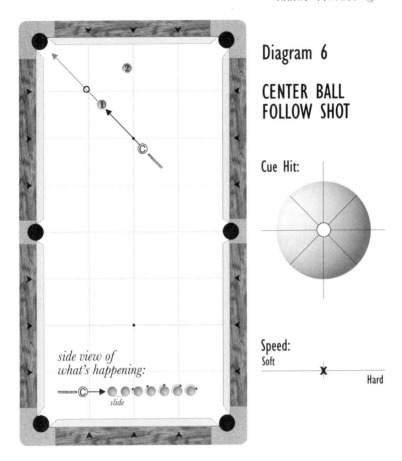

Diagram 6

CENTER BALL FOLLOW SHOT

Cue Hit:

Speed:
Soft ——— x ——— Hard

side view of what's happening:
slide

DRAW SHOT

The draw shot is not easy to learn, but it is impressive. Anytime you can look like you're breaking laws of physics, and you don't even know which laws they are, that's a good thing.

The draw shot seems to defy logic: the cue ball moves forward, strikes the object ball, then reverses and heads back whence it came. It's as if the cue ball has a round-trip ticket. The draw shot is incredibly potent. It opens up the entire table when you know you can sink a shot and bring the cue ball back to set up your next shot.

As I said, however, it is also hard to learn. At least for me it was. I must have had eighty different people try to teach me the draw shot before I finally figured it out.

Now I will combine all of their wisdom into this nugget: *hit the cue ball two cue tips (an inch) below center.*

Your aim is clear. You want the ball to move forward while spinning backward. You are using backspin the same way tennis players do—the shot clears the net, makes contact with the ground, and starts moving back toward you.

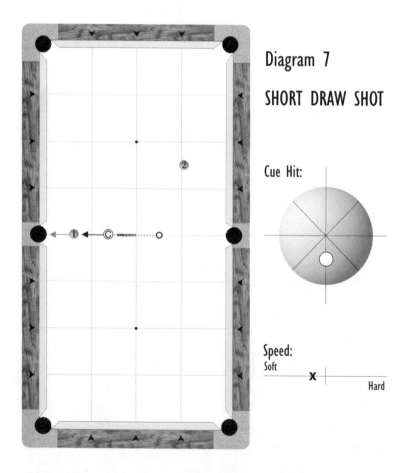

Diagram 7

SHORT DRAW SHOT

Cue Hit:

Speed:

Soft ——— **x** ———| Hard

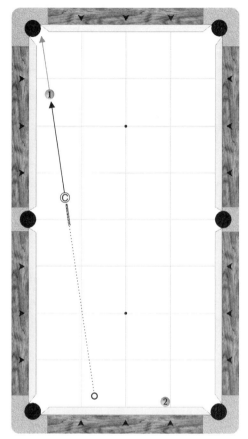

Diagram 8

LONG DRAW SHOT

Cue Hit:

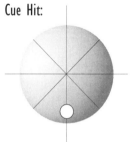

Speed:
Soft ———————————|————— **X**
Hard

Diagram 7 shows a short draw shot. Diagram 8 shows a long draw shot. The concept remains the same, with two slight variations: on the longer shot, hit slightly farther down on the cue ball and use a harder stroke.

It is easy to miscue on the draw shot, because you cannot keep your cue 100 percent level—the rail will get in your way at that height. So chalk up, and elevate the butt of your cue slightly.

My problem was that in an effort to create backspin, I would wind up digging under the ball, sending it jumping into the air. This is not the recipe for a draw shot or a jump shot, but I've learned that it is a good way to look and feel like a fool.

Eventually I learned that I had to give it my full, long stroke and follow-through, but I also had to add some downward motion, which I achieved by elevating the back of my cue.

If you can fully visualize that you want the ball to spin backward, you will be able to execute the shot. I will discuss the phenomenon of visualization in detail later, but it is a golden rule of pool: if you can truly see something in your mind's eye, you can make it happen.

Now that you know how to make the cue ball stop, follow, and come back to you, you're ready to make it dance. Be warned, though—no matter how alluring these techniques are, if you can use the classic center-ball hit, do it. It's the shot with the highest percentage of success, with the least chance of anything going wrong. And while daring has its place, holding the trophy and the winner's check can be pretty satisfying too.

SPECIALTY SHOTS

Do yourself a favor: don't read this chapter.

Go out and play pool instead. Establish your stance, grip, and stroke. Learn how to control the cue ball with the stop, follow, and draw shots. Master those three techniques, so that you know what will happen wherever you hit the cue ball on its vertical axis. Develop your game using those tools until you can run an entire rack.

Then come back and read this chapter to learn about some completely different ways to control the cue ball. But make sure you're ready first. These are powerful tools, but they can completely destroy your game and erode your fundamentals if you try them too early, before you have fully developed your basic skills.

These shots are the equivalent of a curveball for a Little League pitcher. At first, they provide an advantage. But over time, the pitcher who has developed a good, true fastball will build more arm strength, more true power. So think of the long run, and develop your basic game until you can run a rack of balls using only straight-on shots and cut shots. Then, if you are truly ready—and not just kidding yourself—get ready to learn English.

ENGLISH: A SECOND LANGUAGE

English simply means sidespin applied to the cue ball.

Instead of hitting the cue ball dead-center (or high and low, but on the vertical center axis for follow and draw shots), you hit it on either side, as shown in Diagram 9.

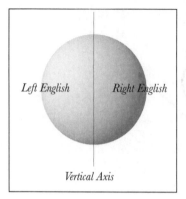

Left English *Right English*

Vertical Axis

Diagram 9

SIDE ENGLISH

English is almost never used to sink an object ball; it is used to determine cue-ball position after your shot. In other words, English is used to set up your next shot.

The effect of the spin is minimal after the cue ball connects with the object ball; it is most pronounced after the cue ball collides with the cushion. Depending on what kind of English you apply, inside or outside, you can increase or decrease the speed and angle at which the cue ball comes off the rail.

Without English, it is easy to predict how the cue ball bounces off the cushion. It is just like your high school geometry teacher insisted: the angle of incidence equals the angle of reflection. If you didn't understand that then, let me make it simple: if a ball goes in at forty-five degrees, it comes out at forty-five degrees.

It's as consistent as McDonald's—you always know what you are going to get. But sometimes that's not what you want. Try taking your wife through the drive-thru on your anniversary, and you'll get the idea.

Sometimes you want the cue ball to do funky things off the rail, so that it will be in a favorable position for your next shot. Of course, you don't just want it to do wild things; you want to control its movement off the rail.

To understand how to achieve this control, you should perform this simple exercise. Clear the table of all object balls. Place the cue ball on the dot where you normally rack the balls. Aim at the side cushion across from you, and stroke the ball dead-center. If you have a steady bridge, comfortable grip, and pendulum stroke, the ball should come right back to you.

Now for the science experiment: reposition the ball and strike it with right English—one cue tip right of center. Notice the rebound: as the ball comes back to you, it heads to your right.

Try it again, but this time stroke the cue ball with left English— just left of center. This time, it will come back to your left.

Keep practicing this, using varying speeds, to get a better feel for the effect English has on a rebounding cue ball.

In game conditions, you can use this to your advantage. When you use what is called running English—the cue ball is spinning in the same direction it will be traveling after contact with the object ball—the English will increase the angle that the ball bounces off

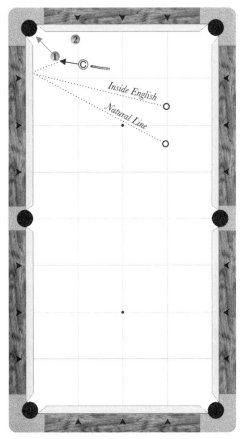

Diagram 10

INSIDE ENGLISH

Cue Hit:

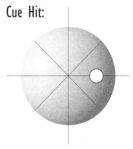

Speed:
Soft
Hard

Use this technique to slow down the cue ball and shorten the angle off the rail.

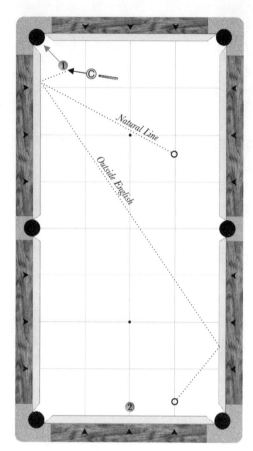

Diagram 11

OUTSIDE ENGLISH

Cue Hit:

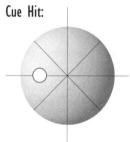

Speed:
Soft ——————X—————— Hard

Use this technique to speed up the cue ball and increase the angle off the rail.

the rail. It also appears to increase the speed of the ball bouncing off the rail, which is why it is known as running English. This is used when you want the cue ball to return toward the center of the table for your next shot.

In contrast, you can use what is known as reverse English—the cue ball is spinning in the opposite direction it will be traveling after contact with the object ball—to shorten the angle and slow the movement of the cue ball off the rail. This is known as killing the cue ball, and you can use it when you want the cue ball to end up near the rail for your next shot.

This all sounds so wonderful—increased cue-ball control opens up more possibilities for longer runs. There are, of course, some drawbacks.

Putting English on the cue ball does affect its path, even before it touches the object ball. It just makes sense; if you hit the ball on the left side, it is going to go not only forward but a little to the right. And vice versa.

This side motion is called deflection, and deflection can make all your aiming go down the drain in a hurry.

When you use English, the amount of deflection increases over long distances. A shot that was imperceptibly off-line over the first few inches will become clearly out of whack as the ball travels several feet. You also get more deflection when you hit the cue ball very slowly.

Deflection is not impossible to overcome, however. That's because the spin you placed on the ball will eventually overcome the force of the sideways push. This is due to the friction between the ball and the cloth—the spinning ball grabs the cloth and slowly spins back into the direction it is spinning.

The trick is to figure out how much spin balances how much deflection for each shot that you line up. Perhaps there is an algorithm out there somewhere, a formula that could help you figure this out. But pool is a social game, and how cool do you think you'll look playing with a calculator? Instead, use your internal calculator—your ability to feel a shot. It takes time, practice, and a willingness to adjust to changing circumstances, but at least there are no batteries required.

Here's one thing to preprogram into your brain: if you hit the cue ball too hard, the spin will never have a chance to overcome the force of the sideways thrust.

Once you've figured out how to balance deflection and spin so that your aim is once again true, you're presented with another problem: throw.

Throw is the word we use to refer to the somewhat wayward path taken by an object ball after it is struck by a cue ball traveling with sidespin, or English. Put simply: the object ball will not react the way it does when struck by a cue ball that is traveling straight. It will be thrown slightly off-line.

At times this can be helpful; you can throw in shots that were otherwise unmakable. But if you do not take it into consideration, it will cause you to miss shots even though you hit the object ball right where you wanted to.

One way to think about it is this: you will transfer English from the cue ball to the object ball. Remember that one aspect of English is deflection. Since the object ball will probably not have enough distance to come spinning back into line, all you have is deflection. So think of throw as the object ball's own deflection.

If you know that when you hit the cue ball with right English you transfer left English onto the object ball, and vice versa, it is easy to figure out which direction you will throw, or deflect, the object ball.

So think ahead, anticipate the off-line movement, and compensate. Remember that, as always, speed is critical. As I mentioned, the harder you hit the cue ball, the less effect your spin will have. This holds true for the spin imparted on the object ball and, hence, the throw, or deflection.

By now your head is probably spinning like a cue ball with some serious English. That is one good reason to use stop, draw, and follow shots and to avoid English whenever possible. There is too much to think about, and too many opportunities for mistakes.

I'm not saying never learn English. I'm saying use it as a last resort.

When you do use English, feel free to combine it with stop, follow, and draw shots. To do that, simply hit the cue ball in the logical place, as demonstrated in Diagrams 12, 13, 14, and 15. For follow with right English, hit the cue ball high right. For follow with left

Diagram 12
HIGH RIGHT ENGLISH

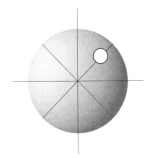

Diagram 13
HIGH LEFT ENGLISH

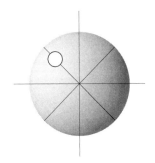

Diagram 14
LOW RIGHT ENGLISH

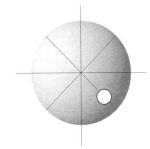

Diagram 15
LOW LEFT ENGLISH

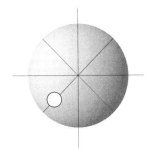

English, hit the cue ball high left. For draw with right English, strike the ball low right. For draw with left English, strike the ball low left.

Take your time, and experiment with these various placements. They seem complicated, but think of the results: if you can master them, you will be able to leave your cue ball anywhere you want. Which will make your next shot easier, and the one after that, and the one after that. . . .

MASSÉ: SO ENGLISH, THEY HAD TO USE A FRENCH WORD

Massé shots are just shots made using extreme English. They can come in handy when you need to hit an object ball that is blocked by another ball, because they allow you to curve the cue ball around obstacles.

They are also extremely tempting to try, because almost every billiard room has a sign saying NO MASSÉ OR JUMP SHOTS. And who can resist bucking authority every once in a while?

Let's try some massé shots. If you are a beginner, you shouldn't even be reading this chapter. But if you are being honest with yourself and you truly have control of your stroke, you shouldn't be afraid of some lousy sign. Especially in a tournament, where you may need a massé shot to win. Of course, there is a risk that you will tear the cloth, ruin the slate table bed, and find yourself with an astronomical bill to pay. So use your judgment.

For a simple massé shot, forget that all-important rule I told you about always keeping your cue level. Instead, elevate the back end between thirty-five and fifty degrees. Keep your hand on the table, and use an open, elevated bridge. This enables you to make the cue ball curve around an eighth or a quarter of a ball that lies between your cue ball and the object ball.

To execute an extreme massé shot, elevate the back end of your cue stick close to ninety degrees—almost straight up in the air!

Now you can see how you could do real damage to the table. That's why I say don't try this at home. Why mess up your own table when you can mess up your friend's table instead? Hee hee.

Having both the cue and your bridge hand in the air can be a little disconcerting. Where is the stability? Massé shots are a little easier if your cue ball is close to the rail, so that you can prop your bridge hand on it. Or for more extreme massés, you can even use a freehand bridge, by bending your bridge arm and tucking your

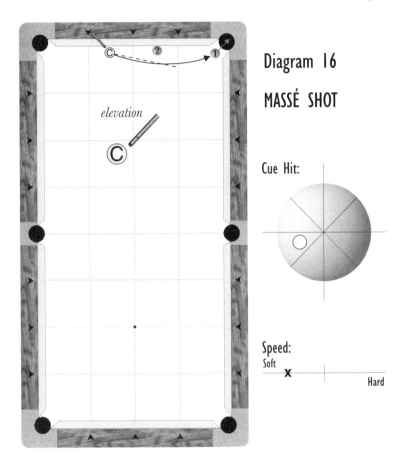

Diagram 16

MASSÉ SHOT

Cue Hit:

Speed:
Soft

Hard

bridge elbow against your side. You can use an open or closed bridge. I use open for massés when my hand is on the table, and a closed bridge for freehand massés. This is legal, as long as one foot remains on the floor.

Now you can brace your bridge arm against your side. As for the grip hand, just make sure it is comfortable. You don't have to use the standard grip if it does not feel right. Some people hold the cue with a closed fist, as if they were about to go spearfishing. For massé shots, that's fine. It's the result that counts.

As you look down on the cue ball, just imagine you are looking at a clock face. It's just been turned on its side. Now, you definitely don't want to hit it dead-center—that would drive the ball into the table and could shatter your cue.

It also won't do you much good to hit the ball above center— that would send the ball back toward you. So hit it low, either to the left or the right of center. The ball will travel in a half circle—out to the side, and then back to hit the object ball.

Notice that the softer you hit the ball, the sooner it will curve out and come back in again. When you hit it harder, it will go farther out before returning.

The biggest mistake people make when shooting massé shots is shooting them too hard. As you're aiming, try to find a spot just to the left or just to the right of the obstructing ball. Pick a spot on the table. Note your errors and adjust your aim accordingly.

Now you know one trick for getting around a ball that is clearly in your way. That knowledge should limit the number of times you walk up to the table and say, "Oh, you left me no shot."

JUMP SHOT

There is, of course, another way to overcome a ball blocking your path to the desired object ball—go over it.

You'll see on television that a lot of us have special jump cues designed just for this purpose. These cues are smaller and shorter than a regular cue, and they enable us to more easily generate the speed we need to execute the jump shot.

You can, however, do a jump shot with a regular cue. You have to elevate your cue, similar to the position for a basic massé shot. A forty-five-degree angle should do it.

Establish an elevated open bridge as well, so that you are aiming down on the cue ball from above.

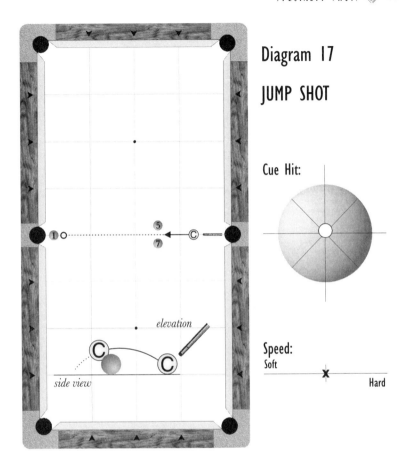

Diagram 17

JUMP SHOT

Cue Hit:

Speed:
Soft   **X**   **Hard**

elevation

side view

Don't get greedy and try to leap over an entire ball—Evel Knievel didn't try to jump Snake Canyon his first time out. Instead, use this shot when only part of the ball is in your way, and leap over the side of the ball, where it is not quite as tall. The ball that you are jumping should be between twelve and eighteen inches from the cue ball.

The object ball should be straight ahead of the cue ball, and you want to hit it straight on. For most players, it is just too tough to jump a ball, then precisely cut the object ball. Only if you are confident with your jumping ability should you try to do a jump shot that asks for a thin cut on the object ball.

Now that you've got the shot set up, you're ready to give it a try. Absolutely do not try to scoop the ball off the cloth. It doesn't work; you have no control over the cue ball, and it is a foul that allows your opponent to shoot from wherever on the table he or she wants to.

Instead, shoot down, hard and fast, on top of the ball. You are driving the ball down into the slate, and it will jump up in response.

You don't have to be musclebound to execute a jump shot. You need speed, so that your stroke acts like a whip cracking. Obviously, you don't have the normal follow-through—where would it go? Instead, snap down, pull the cue back, and watch the ball take off like Superman.

Once you get the hang of the jump shot, the cue ball will jump over the obstacle ball and hit the table and the object ball at the same instant. The cue ball will roll slightly forward or slightly back, the object ball will head toward the pocket, and your opponent's jaw just might hit the floor.

YOU ALWAYS HAVE A SHOT

I love stepping up to the table when it looks like I don't have a shot. To everyone else, it may look hopeless, but to me it is always a challenge to see how deep into my arsenal I can reach.

To me, it's a creative act, and it's a big part of what makes a player able to improve quickly. When there are no clear shots, don't just shrug your shoulders—exercise your brain and look for a bank shot or a killer safety.

Take a deep breath, think, and reevaluate the situation. Even if the table appears to be an unsolvable puzzle, relax. I am going to show you a variety of shots lurking beneath the surface. Bank shots are hard to notice sometimes, and they are almost always hard to execute, until you have practiced them over and over again.

Yet they will give you the advantage you need to beat someone who can see the table only in a superficial way. They enable you to go beyond the obvious, into your imagination. . . .

BANK SHOTS

On a bank shot, you make the cue ball hit the object ball so that the object ball collides with a rail before traveling to the intended pocket.

Try not to take a bank shot when you have a straight-on or cut shot you can make. Bank shots may look cool, but they are extremely difficult to master. On a traditional shot, all you have to worry about is making sure the cue ball reaches the aiming point on the object ball. On bank shots, that's just the beginning. Even if you connect with the object ball at precisely the right point, there is no guarantee that you will make your shot.

That is because there are so many potentially troubling factors. A geometry student assumes that the cue ball bounces off the rail at the same angle it approaches. This is a good guide—perhaps a better guide than any of the involved systems I will describe—but it is only a guide.

The problem with this theory is that you may be dealing with a rail that has some dead spots. Or you may have hit the ball too hard or too soft, which will affect the angle at which the ball comes off the rail.

For these reasons, another shot that looks quite difficult may in fact be easier than a simple-looking bank shot.

Nevertheless, you will come across situations in which you'll need to make a bank shot.

When I am faced with this situation, I use what is called the mirror system. The mirror system takes a little imagination. You have to picture another table, connected to yours like a pair of hotel beds pushed together.

Let's say you want to bank a ball off the far rail and into the side pocket near where you are standing. Simple. Imagine the second table extending beyond the end of the actual table you are playing on. Can you see exactly where the second table's far side pocket is? If you can, aim directly for it. The cue ball will bank off the rail and sink into the real side pocket closest to you.

Obviously, your ball will not go flying off the table and land in the imaginary pocket. If you have pictured the mirror table correctly, the ball will hit the far side rail and return to the pocket nearest you, as shown in Diagram 18.

The same system works for long shots into the corners. It may take more practice to conjure up the pocket, simply because it will be farther away, but the principle is the same.

If you are searching for a more concrete method of sinking bank shots, make this one adjustment to your preshot routine: walk around the table and look at your shot from the opposite perspective. From there, you should be able to easily establish where on the cushion you want the object ball to hit. Then walk back around and aim for the ball to hit that spot. Pay attention to each step of your results. Did you hit the spot you wanted? If not, work on your aim. If you hit the spot you wanted but the object ball did not go to the intended pocket, you may have lined the shot up incorrectly. Next time, adjust.

These techniques work for me. Knowing that with a medium hit, center-ball stroke, the angle in equals the angle out is usually

Diagram 18

MIRROR SYSTEM OF BANKING

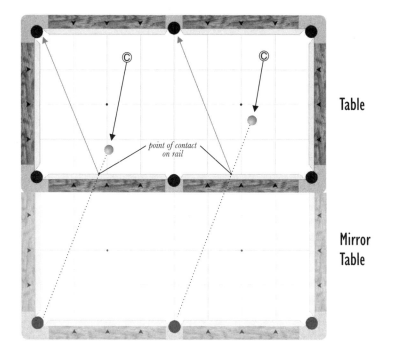

point of contact
on rail

Table

Mirror
Table

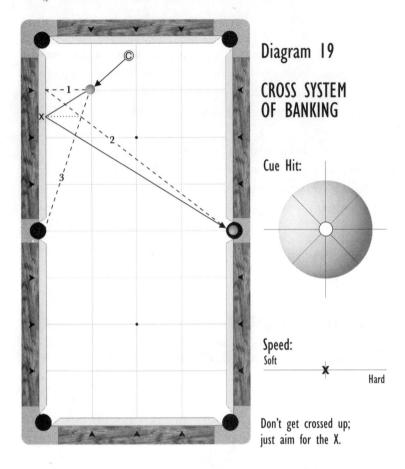

Diagram 19

CROSS SYSTEM OF BANKING

Cue Hit:

Speed:
Soft ——————X—————— Hard

Don't get crossed up; just aim for the X.

good enough. If I need a system, I'll fall back on the mirror system. When I need to measure my shot, I walk around to the far side of the table, and then I know just what to do.

Yet for some players, none of these tactics get the job done. Many players use what is known as the cross system, which is illustrated in Diagram 19.

Stand facing the object ball. Draw a line straight from the object ball to the far rail, and notice its arrival point. Now draw a second line, from that point to the pocket where you want to sink the ball. Now draw a third line (all these lines are in your head, not chalked on the table) from the object ball to the pocket *opposite* the one you want the ball to wind up in. Don't get crossed up; just aim for the X that marks the spot on the far wall across from where lines 2 and 3 intersect. Note carefully the point where these two lines intersect. From that point, draw a line straight to the cushion. That's where you need the object ball to hit in order to sink your shot.

Now you can see why I prefer the other techniques. In pool, as in science, the simplest solution is the most satisfying. I don't want to be drawing an imaginary cat's cradle on the pool table in the middle of my match. It's not fun, and I don't see the point of playing if it's not fun.

I'd rather trust my judgment. The only use I can see for having a complicated system is this: when you get nervous, your feel for the game is the first thing that goes. So in a pressure situation like that, it may feel good to know you have a system behind you. If you've still got the wherewithal to figure it out.

Otherwise, trust yourself, your vision, and your feel for the table. It should be enough.

PLAYING GAMES

STRAIGHT POOL

Straight pool is my favorite game. The classic old-timers' game, it's also known as 14.1-continuous, because you sink fourteen out of fifteen balls before reracking and continuing to play.

This is the first game I learned how to play, and I still think it is the best way to learn how to play pool. It teaches you the importance of accuracy and touch, concentration and cue-ball control.

My old mentor, Gene Nagy, is a retired professional who lives in Queens with his folks. He rolls his own tobacco, flies kites and model airplanes in his spare time, and has a way of making life seem simple.

He never taught me anything directly, never corrected my stroke or told me how to do something at the table. He never let me in on any shortcuts, no matter how much I begged him. Instead, he'd just ask, "Jeanette, ya ready?"

And that's how it was, from the beginning. We were playing a game.

Before I met him, I was always panicking about one thing or another. Whether it was this tournament, or that shot I couldn't master, or a fight with my family, or a breakup with a boyfriend, there was always some issue.

Like most pool players, I was my own worst enemy, sabotaging any gains I made by constantly wondering why I wasn't getting better faster.

Gene allowed me to just play. He was always there for me, day after day, looking at me with his wise eyes with the giant bags underneath, just nodding and playing, nodding and playing.

It made me love the game more than I ever had.

So that's my advice to you: just play. Here's how.

To start a game of straight pool, my favorite game of all time, rack up fifteen balls at the table's foot spot and lag to see who breaks. In straight pool, the rules are that you can shoot any ball on the table at any time, but you must call the ball and the pocket you are aiming for. Therefore, the player who wins the lag should choose not to break, because the chances of sinking a called shot off the break are

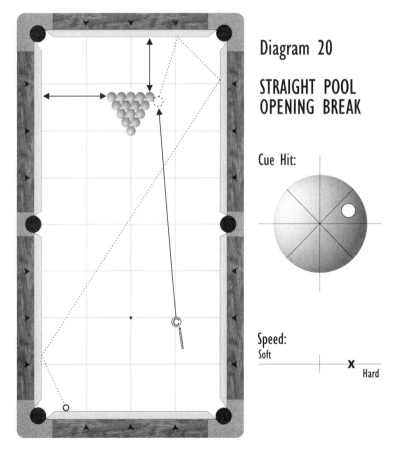

Diagram 20

STRAIGHT POOL
OPENING BREAK

Cue Hit:

Speed:
Soft

X
Hard

slim. It is more likely that you'll just end up leaving an easy shot for your opponent. If you must break, try to hit the cue ball so that you leave your opponent with no easy shots. The best way to achieve that is shown in Diagram 20. Hit the cue ball high right, medium hard, and aim for the ball at the back right corner of the triangle as if to sink it in the far left pocket. This should send that ball to the far rail and then back toward the rack. The ball at the back left corner should head for the side cushion and also bounce back toward the pack. The cue ball will bound off three rails and come to rest along the end rail closest to you.

The rules require that on the break you drive two or more object balls and the cue ball to a rail. If you scratch the cue ball into a pocket on the break without hitting two balls into the rail, you lose two points, and your opponent can make you break again. All other scratches or fouls cost one point, and any balls pocketed on a scratch are pulled and placed on the foot spot. If you commit fouls on three consecutive shots, you lose sixteen points—one for the foul, and 15 for having done it three times in a row.

Every called ball is worth one point, and any other balls sunk on a called shot are worth one additional point each. The game is over when one player reaches a predetermined point total. Almost everybody races to 100 or 150 points. I like to play to 1,000. I may be the only person in the world who actually enjoys this. After a thirteen-hour race to 1,000, I sometimes ask my partner if he wants to extend the game to 1,200.

Usually he'll roll his eyes and mumble something about having to get home.

For me, though, straight pool is the greatest game on earth. You break safe—not smashing the balls all over the table but gently nudging the rack so that the cue ball and two object balls touch a rail—and this leaves almost all the object balls on one end of the table, with the cue ball down at the other end.

That arrangement takes almost all the power out of the game.

What is left is pure beauty: finesse, creativity, originality, and touch. With so many balls gathered in such a small area, you will quickly learn how valuable accuracy and cue-ball control can be.

When you're a beginner, there is no better game to help you develop your skills. Playing straight pool will improve your position play, touch, composure, decision making, concentration, and stamina.

It's not like nine-ball, where if you fall asleep for a moment the game is over, and you have a chance to reenergize yourself for the next one. Straight pool is one long game, so you had better shoot well from the outset. If you start slow, you had better get your game together quick, or you will be forced to endure a long, humiliating pummeling. In straight pool, you can miss a shot and find yourself sitting down for a very, very long time.

The object of straight pool is simply to sink more balls than your opponent. The only way to do that is to go on long runs, during which you pocket ball after ball without missing. You play to a mutually agreed upon number of points, normally 100 or 150.

Yet unless you master some simple strategies, your runs will never rise above fourteen balls.

There are two balls you have to focus on in order to extend your runs. The first is known as the key ball, which will be the second to last ball remaining on the table. When you sink this ball, you want to be sure that you have good position on the next ball, which is known as the break ball.

The break ball is the ball that truly determines your ability to extend your run. That is because when one ball is left on the table, your opponent reracks the other fourteen balls, to keep the game going.

Once the balls are racked, you want to sink the break ball and have the cue ball carom into the rack, spreading out the balls so that you have another shot. This is not so hard to execute, if you have planned in advance where your break ball will be.

That is the secret to winning straight pool. When your turn begins, you should examine the entire table and select in your mind the key ball and the break ball. The break ball should be near the point where the balls will be reracked once the table is all but empty.

After you've selected your break ball and key ball, work backward. You know that the break ball will be last and the key ball will be the one just before it. Now devise a pattern that will get you around the table, in position for those two final shots.

Don't expect to be able to map all of this out the very first time you play. It takes a lot of practice. But if you do not attempt it, you will never be able to make lengthy runs. You will always find yourself limited by bad position on one or both of the final balls.

There are, of course, other hazards that can thwart you long before you reach those balls. You may find several balls clinging together in clusters, or balls that are frozen against the rail, or balls blocking other balls from going into the pocket.

I always try to eliminate these trouble areas as quickly as possible. They make it difficult to plan ahead, because so many bad things can happen while they are still on the table. If you just try to avoid them, they may wind up as your key ball or break shot, and you certainly don't want that.

As for the clusters, they may not be as troublesome as they appear. Sometimes balls will be frozen together not far from a pocket, which will give you an easy shot at one of them. Otherwise, break them up gently; don't give in to the temptation just to whack them around. With so many balls in so little space, they are bound to wind up forming new clusters.

To take care of the blocking balls, try to sink them first. If that seems impossible, gently bump them into a new position, either with the cue ball or an object ball, so that on your next turn you will have a clean look at the pocket.

Even after you have cleared all these hurdles, it is not enough to simply play aggressively and try to make every ball you can. Safety play is very important in straight pool. Safety play is just another term for defense—shooting a shot not to sink a ball but only to make sure that your opponent does not have a good shot when she comes to the table. As with other shots, you must call a safety shot in advance, and either the cue ball or a colored ball must hit a rail—otherwise you have committed a foul, and you lose one point.

In some games, safety play is fairly easy, because you only have to stop your opponent from shooting one or two designated balls. In straight pool, it is quite difficult, because your opponent can shoot any ball she wants. Finding a safety that leaves her no makable shot thus becomes extremely difficult.

One option is leaving the cue ball at the far end of the table. Since all the balls should be gathered at the near end, this at least forces her to try to sink a long shot. This tactic is especially effective against less skilled and less experienced players. If you can freeze the cue ball against the far cushion, so much the better. She will then be forced to take a long shot, using a rail bridge and a follow stroke—no easy task.

There will be times when you want to "back-scratch," or intentionally commit a foul. Every time you do, it will cost you one point, but it could be worth it if you are faced with a situation where trying to hit a legal shot that would drive a ball to a rail would open up a cluster and provide a series of easy shots for your opponent. In these circumstances, gently nudging the cue ball into the cluster might be the lesser of two evils.

To decide how offensively or defensively you want to play, you have to know your own game. Honestly and objectively appraise your skill level, and do not go for shots that you have little or no chance of making. If you don't have a shot that you are confident you can make and still set up another shot, play safe.

I could go on and on about the game, but the best way to learn it is to play it. Don't listen to people who say straight pool is dead; it is still the best way to improve as a player, and to me, it is the purest form of the sport.

CRAZY EIGHTS

Eight-ball is a very popular game, but I never play it because I compete in nine-ball. To me, nine-ball is an explosive sprint, while eight-ball is a leisurely jog. People like eight-ball because it is very straightforward: stripes versus solids, with the 8-ball waiting around till the end.

You may encounter different house rules depending on where you play, but the basic idea is that one player shoots at balls 1–7 (solids) and the other shoots at 9–15 (stripes). You must hit one of your own balls first, but you do not have to call any shots, except the 8-ball.

After the break, you cannot sink the 8-ball until after you have made all your assigned balls. Once you have cleared the table of all your balls, you can shoot the 8-ball, but if you scratch or put it in the wrong pocket, you lose. When that player shoots the 8-ball into the pocket she called, she wins.

Eight-ball has its advantages. It's a good game for four people to play, with two on a team, each team member alternating turns at the table. It also lasts a while, because the other team's balls are often blocking your own, so it's good to play on a coin-operated table at a bar, where you pay per game, not per minute.

One common mistake: when people make a plan on how to run out and then their balls get out of line, they frequently try to force their predetermined plan onto the new circumstances. It doesn't work. You have to be willing to adapt to the situation at hand. It's like you've got a road atlas and you're crossing eight states—you make a plan, but once you're on the road and hit a roadblock or a detour, you've got to get the map out again and make a whole new route. Otherwise you'll never get there.

There are several keys to winning eight-ball. First, develop a monster break shot that scatters balls and dumps at least one or two into the pockets. This gives you control of the table, because the first player to sink a ball gets to choose whether she wants to be solids or stripes.

There are two effective ways to break in eight-ball. The first, shown in Diagram 21, is called the controlled eight-ball break. Hit the cue ball hard and in the center, aiming dead-on at the head ball. Your object is to scatter the colored balls widely and have the cue ball come to rest in a central position. Strike the cue ball hard center, and use a long follow-through. Focus on hitting the head ball squarely. The rack will scatter, and the cue ball should return to the center of the table, within the dotted box.

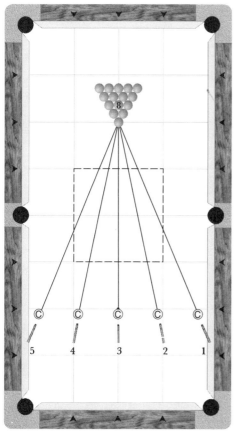

Diagram 21

CONTROLLED EIGHT-BALL BREAK

Cue Hit:

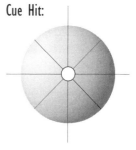

Speed:
Soft
Hard

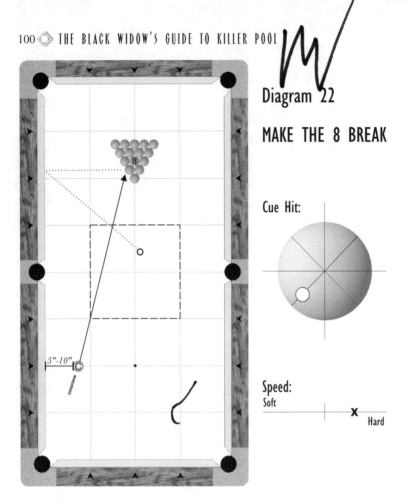

Diagram 22

MAKE THE 8 BREAK

Cue Hit:

Speed:
Soft

X
Hard

The second, more aggressive break, shown in Diagram 22, is designed to make the 8-ball and win the game. You should strike the cue ball medium-hard and aim for the second ball in the rack. Use bottom-left English. The 8-ball is always racked in the middle of the triangle in this game, and you have a decent chance of sending it into one of the side pockets. Unfortunately, if you don't sink the 8, you have very little cue-ball control to set up your next shot.

Even if you pocket a solid or a stripe on the break, you don't have to choose to go after that type of ball. Take your time and decide wisely. Rather than choosing the first easy shot you see, look for which group has the most balls within close range of the pockets. If you can see an easier path to victory using the other kind of balls, go for it. This is probably the most important decision you will make in a game of eight-ball, because it will determine all of your following shots.

When you are trying to run the table in eight-ball, try not to break up any clusters that could cause problems for your opponent. Let them be, and make your opponent clean up her own mess.

Try to get rid of your trouble areas as soon as possible. If you work around them and leave yourself nothing but a cluster, when you break them up you might have no shot left, and, since it's later in the game, your opponent will have a clear table. If you focus on your clusters from the outset, even if you make a mistake the table will be crowded, your opponent will be unlikely to run out, and you can return to the table with a chance to run the rack.

When you break up these clusters that form your trouble spots, don't just fire away with the cue ball. Make a shot in such a way that the cue ball will break up the cluster after pocketing the object ball. Be sure you have a backup ball for your next shot, because you can't be sure of where the dislodged balls will end up.

Some people claim that it is weak to play defense during an eight-ball game in a bar. I say let them be the hero—they may think otherwise when they're paying for the next game and racking up the balls.

NINE-BALL

Nine-ball is by far the sexiest game.

It is perfect for television; it is fast moving, the table is wide open, and it provides plenty of opportunities to put spin on the cue ball.

It is also the game that puts gas in my Jaguar.

The game starts with just nine balls racked on the table: the balls numbered 1 through 9.

The name of the game is the same as its object: pocket the

9-ball. Nothing else matters. You can pocket balls 1 through 8, but if your opponent sinks the 9 on a legal shot, the game is hers.

Yet there is one factor complicating things. In nine-ball, you must always strike the lowest-numbered ball on the table first. You don't have to sink that ball, but you must hit it first.

This opens up the game for aggressive play. Let's say the 1-, 2-, and 3-balls have been pocketed. You have to hit the 4-ball first, but if you can see a makable combination, using the 4 to pocket the 9, you can win the game right there.

At the start of the game, the balls are racked tightly together in a diamond formation. Some people buy special plastic nine-ball racks, but I recommend a good sturdy wooden rack designed to hold fifteen balls. That way, you can put your fingers in it and really make sure the balls are racked together snugly. Otherwise, the balls won't spread over the table when they're hit; they'll just bounce around off one another, then lollygag a couple of inches away. For me, racking in a plastic rack is like trying to pack water into a plastic bag; it just keeps changing its shape.

The break is the most important shot in nine-ball. If the 9-ball goes in on the break on a perfect rack, you win; but I am convinced that is just pure luck. The reason the break is so important is because it can give you control of the table.

See Diagram 23 for efficient nine-ball breaks. The best breaks in nine-ball spread the rack, pocket balls, and leave you with control of the cue ball. The harder you can break with accuracy, the better. I put so much energy into my break that I look like I'm rising up out of my shoes.

Anytime after the break, if you scratch in the pocket or you don't hit the ball you're aiming for, your opponent gets the cue ball in hand. That means he can shoot from anywhere on the table, and it often means he will run the rack, so be careful.

Remember, you only have to sink nine balls, not fifteen, so control of the table gives you a decent chance to run out the game with-

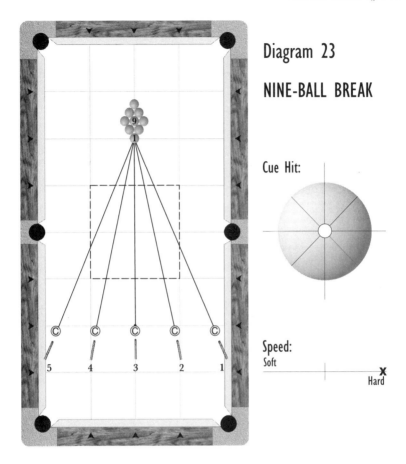

Diagram 23

NINE-BALL BREAK

Cue Hit:

Speed:
Soft

Hard

out your opponent ever shooting. When you break, it is important that you keep control of the cue ball—don't let it run all over the place, because if you scratch, your opponent could run out, and it'll be all over for you. So when you break, try to get the cue ball to hit the 1-ball as solidly as possible, so it will roll off about a foot and stop. This is called "squatting whitey" or "killing your rock."

Watch where the cue ball goes. If it follows forward, you're hitting too high on the cue ball; if it rolls all the way back toward you, you're hitting too low. Compensate.

Also pay attention to where the 1-ball goes. The 1-ball should go in the side pocket opposite to where you're breaking from. If it doesn't go in, it should bank off the rail near that side pocket and move toward the corner pocket that you are standing in front of. This should give you a decent shot and a chance to start a run.

Immediately after the break, and before any other legal shot, you are allowed to do what is called a "push-out" if you cannot see the 1-ball. You can shoot the cue ball anywhere on the table and it can hit any ball, or none at all, as long as it does not go in a pocket. Your opponent then has the option to shoot the shot you've left for him or to make you shoot again. You want to leave it so he has a shot at the 1-ball, but it is a very difficult, low-percentage shot that will not leave him with a good position should he manage to pocket the ball.

Nine-ball is not the most complex game on earth, but you do need to develop a strategy based on your own abilities. If you are good enough to run the table, then play strictly offensively. Nine-ball is an aggressive game, and there are no points awarded for meekness.

However, if you cannot run out the table, either because you are not yet good enough or there are unmanageable trouble spots, pick the right time to make a safety.

Don't wait too long if you're going to have to shoot a safety. If you sink all the balls up until the 7 or the 8 before shooting a safety, you are leaving a pretty open table. If your safety fails, your turn is over, the table is wide open, and your opponent may be just one or two shots away from victory. So plan ahead.

Nine-ball is a great chance to use your whole bag of tricks—English, massé shots, even jump shots. Tune in to ESPN and you will see us playing nine-ball, at least once a week. It is not just fun to watch, it is informative. The cameras catch all the angles, and the commentators explain our thought processes pretty well. That way, you can see everything I'm talking about in action.

TRICK SHOTS

I had been playing pool for about a year when I saw my first trick-shot exhibition. It was given by this guy, Dr. Cue (Tom Rossman), who traveled around doing corporate exhibitions and shows at universities and colleges.

I was spending a semester at the University of Buffalo and my friends and I filed into the auditorium, eager to be wowed. But Dr. Cue missed his first couple of shots and I got cynical pretty fast. Please, I thought, give me a break. You can set up these shots any way you want, and you still can't make 'em?

I thought of my few experiences in tournament play and decided that I had shot much tougher shots in those situations, where I had no control over the lay of the table.

Dr. Cue ended up putting on a great show, though, with a lot of jokes, and by the end he was making all of his trick shots.

Still, I thought I was the real expert—until I tried some trick shots myself. Turns out they are a heck of a lot harder than anything you'll be forced to shoot during a match. In competition, it's pretty simple: find your target, let the shot go, and sink it.

For trick shots, there are many more variables. You're dealing with multiple balls and multiple rails, the newness and cleanliness of the cloth and balls, the speed of the cloth, the tightness of the rails to the table, the humidity, and even the temperature in the room.

You're also hitting a lot of combinations, so you have to take into account the transfer of spin from one ball to another. In the end, it's not just about the setup. It's about setting it up right and hitting the cue ball at the right speed, with the right amount of English and with true accuracy.

By now, I have developed tremendous respect for Dr. Cue and anyone else with enough courage to put on trick-shot exhibitions. I especially admire Mike Massey's work—I have learned a lot from his shows and videotapes. I have done hundreds of exhibitions myself, for charities, at Fortune 500 seminars, and at university gatherings, and I have learned just how hard it is to have everything go right.

No matter how many times I've tried a shot, I am never completely sure it's going to work. Last year I went on *The Late Late Show* with Craig Kilborn and did a handful of trick shots with about fifteen million people watching.

Luckily, my tricks went over. I even managed to teach him a quick trick, and he hit it pretty well.

Trick shots can be scary, but they can also be great fun. They are a light part of the game that can break up tension and frustration, and they are always good for impressing your friends and neighbors. So try the shots diagrammed on the following pages. I suggest you practice them first before trying to show off, so you can see for yourself how tough they really are.

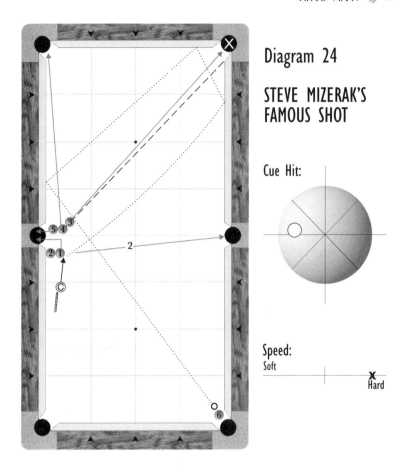

Diagram 24

STEVE MIZERAK'S FAMOUS SHOT

Cue Hit:

Speed:
Soft

X
Hard

This is the first trick shot I ever learned. Set up the balls as shown, making sure that balls 1 and 2 are frozen to each other, exactly perpendicular to the rail. The 3, 4, and 5 should also be frozen together. The 4 and 5 are perpendicular to the rail, and the 3 and 4 should point toward the pocket marked X. Strike the cue ball hard, with left English.

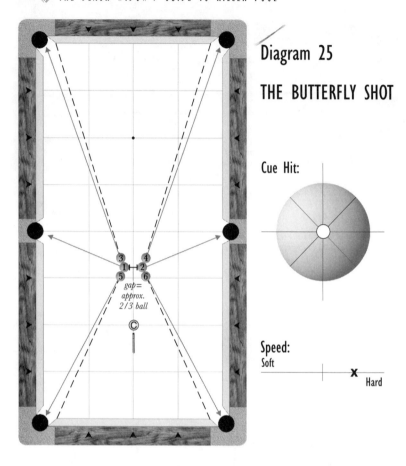

Diagram 25

THE BUTTERFLY SHOT

Cue Hit:

Speed:
Soft

x

Hard

Just set up the table as shown, strike the cue ball hard, dead-center, and watch the shot sprout wings. Make sure to aim the 1 and 3, 2 and 4, 1 and 5, and the 2 and 6 toward the dotted lines.

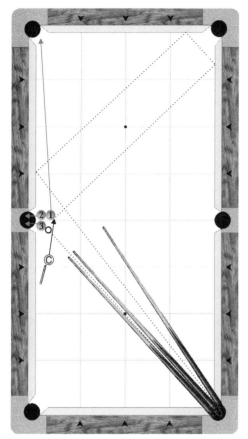

Diagram 26

THE RAILROAD SHOT

Cue Hit:

Speed:
Soft
                                    x
                                        Hard

The cue ball is the engine and the object balls are the boxcars. The engine (cue ball) is going to deliver the two boxcars (object balls 1 and 2) to their home depots. Then the engine is going to go around the country. Take three cue sticks of equal length and jam their butts into the lower-right corner pocket. The two cues on the left are close together, facing the left side pocket. Freeze the 1 and 2 together, perpendicular to the rail. Using high left English, aim to hit the outer edge of the 1-ball as indicated with a medium-hard stroke. This one takes practice, because if your speed is off, the cue ball will never make it up and around the railroad tracks.

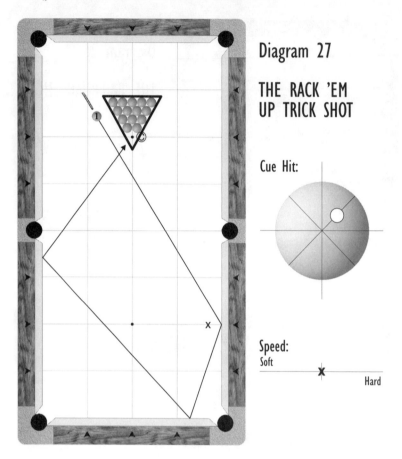

Diagram 27

THE RACK 'EM UP TRICK SHOT

Cue Hit:

Speed:
Soft ——————X—————— Hard

This is the perfect way to dazzle an opponent right before the game starts. Set up fourteen balls in the rack, place the 1-ball close beside it, and place the cue ball underneath the triangle, propping it up. Hit the 1-ball at 2:30 on the clock face with medium force toward the spot marked X. The ball bounces off three cushions, comes up the table, and knocks the cue ball out of the way as it settles into the rack. Look nonchalant, then break.

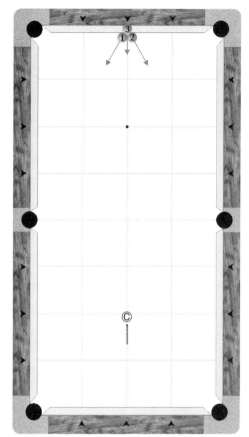

Diagram 28

THE SLOW-COLLAPSE

Cue Hit:

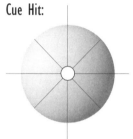

Speed:
Soft
x
Hard

Place two balls frozen to the foot rail at the middle diamond. Take the 3-ball and put it on top of the foot rail so that it leans against the other two balls. Tell your friends, "I bet I can make my cue ball hit the 3-ball without touching the 1 or 2." They'll laugh in your face, until you shoot the cue ball straight in between the 1 and the 2. As the cue ball approaches, bump the table with your hip.

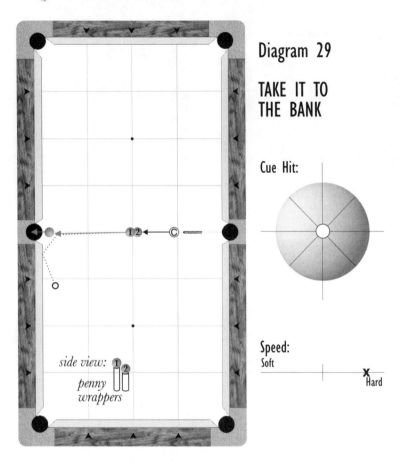

Diagram 29

TAKE IT TO THE BANK

Cue Hit:

Speed:
Soft

X
Hard

side view:
penny
wrappers

You'll need a pair of empty penny wrappers. Cut one of them so it's only two-thirds as high as the other. Set the 1- and 2-ball on top of the wrappers in the center of the table directly in line with each side pocket. The balls should be frozen to each other. Make sure the lower ball is closest to you. Place a third ball in front of the side pocket farthest from you. Shoot the cue ball through the penny wrappers, pocketing the third ball in such a way that the cue ball moves out of the way. The 1- and 2-balls will drop simultaneously, bounce off each other, and split into opposite side pockets.

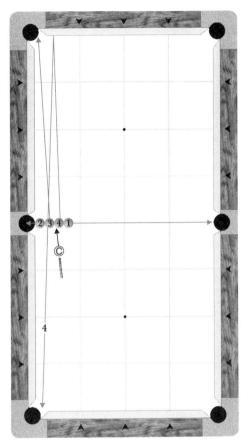

Diagram 30

FOUR IN A ROW

Cue Hit:

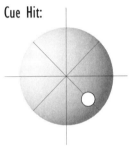

Speed:
Soft

X
Hard

Start by placing four balls frozen together in a row in front of the side pocket. By hitting the cue ball hard with bottom-right English and aiming directly between the center balls, you should be able to drive all four balls into separate pockets.

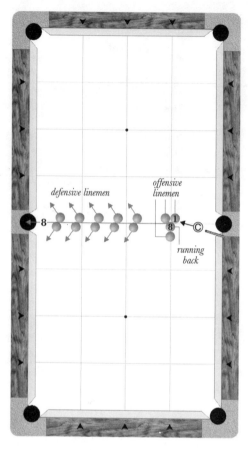

Diagram 31

THE FOOTBALL SHOT

Cue Hit:

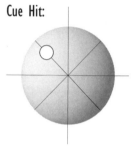

Speed:
Soft ———————————— X ———— Hard

Hut, hut, hike! Line up the balls as shown, with the cue ball as the running back starting from the edge of the side pocket. The three closest balls represent the offensive linemen, while the other ten are defensive linemen. Make sure they are frozen to each other. Using a fluid stroke, strike the cue ball at 10:30, and aim to hit the 1-ball on the left side so that the cue ball caroms off onto the 8-ball. You might have a few false starts on this one, but when you finally score a touchdown, you'll be dancing in the end zone.

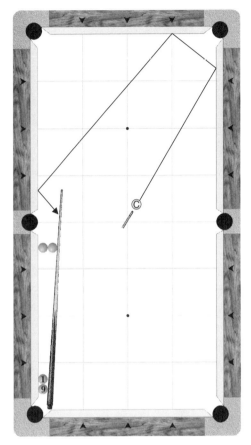

Diagram 32

SNAKE IN THE GRASS

Cue Hit:

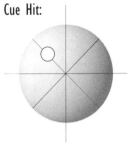

Speed:
Soft ———————— x ————————— Hard

Look out below—someone's about to get bit. Set up the table as shown and announce that you are going to pocket the 9-ball without jumping the cue stick, touching the other two balls, or knocking it in with the cue. While your friends are still scratching their heads, strike the cue ball at 10:30 with a medium stroke. It'll hit three rails, then move the cue stick just enough to avoid hitting the two balls before sliding down the side of the cue like a snake to pocket the 1-9 combination!

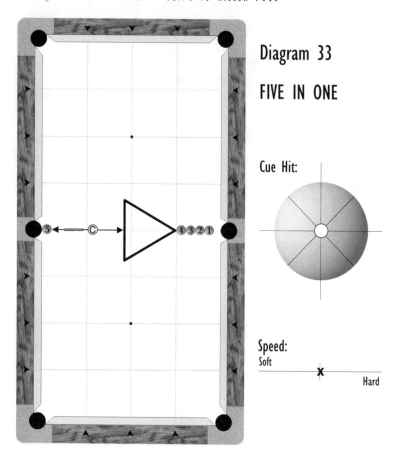

Diagram 33

FIVE IN ONE

Cue Hit:

Speed:
Soft   X
                Hard

Set up four object balls in a line facing the side pocket, as shown. Lay the triangle so its point touches the last of the four balls. Hit the cue ball dead-center, with a medium stroke, right into the center of the rack. It should pocket all four balls in the side pocket, then bounce back to sink the fifth in the opposite side pocket.

HOW TO WIN

12 POOL ETIQUETTE

Some of my professional opponents might claim that I have no right to tell anyone how to behave while playing pool.

I mean, should Dennis Rodman teach people manners?

Still, you need to know some of the ways to behave in competitive settings, and I plan to warn you in advance. Besides, I think some of those players are just clinging to an old misperception of me.

See, when I first joined the tour, I got a bad rap in a hurry. I was accused of being a poor sport, but really I was just a novice then, twenty-one years old, and no one had bothered to tell me how to behave in a professional setting.

When I got hot under the lights, I flipped my hair. When I missed a shot, I stamped my feet and shouted. I made glowering faces that gave the impression that I wanted to murder my opponent.

I was ambitious and far from humble. I carried myself with confidence and drew a lot of media attention, probably before I was ready for it. The other players resented this, and, to be honest, it wasn't all coming to me because I played well. I stood out from the other women—I was the youngest woman on tour, the only Asian, and the most fashion-conscious player. For better or worse, I caught the media's eye.

When reporters asked me what I wanted out of the sport, I told them I wanted to be the best. I said, I want to stomp these other women, so they'd better get out of my way.

I know, it's not exactly the way you're supposed to talk as a rookie. Rookies are supposed to be like busboys, seen and not heard. But I remember Allen Iverson, his first year, saying he refused to respect Michael Jordan on the court. And I think that, in a way, he is right. If you respect your opponent too much, you'll never beat him.

That doesn't mean that I never said nice things about the players during my interviews. I mean, let's be real. These women had been my idols for years. I always told reporters, "I'm thrilled to be here with these great players," and "I really respect the women who have played so well for so many years."

Strangely enough, these quotes never made it into the articles. They just weren't sexy enough, I guess. The stories painted me as a vamp and a killer, like some sort of *Melrose Place* villain come to life. The *New York Times Magazine* called me "a bad Bond girl."

A lot of times, people came to believe that I was this caricature, because they only saw me in killer mode at the table. We never went for coffee or hung out at the hotels, where they would have had a chance to see the lighter side of my personality.

I quickly became a pariah. I didn't have many friends on the tour, only acquaintances. Part of me dreaded going to the events, because I knew that I would wind up alone in my hotel room, crying over the phone to my true friends back home.

I've grown up a lot since then. I know more about how to deal with the other players and the press, and how to handle myself at tournaments. But some things haven't changed—the World Nine-Ball Championship isn't a Miss Congeniality contest sponsored by Martha Stewart. And I'm not out there looking to make friends. I'm still looking to kick butt and take names.

By now, the other professionals respect me. But I'm not convinced it is because I changed. I think that they just grew to accept me once I backed up my talk. Now I'm a veteran. But I don't make the new players coming up go through what I went through, because I just don't think it's fair. When new players come on the tour, I make sure to welcome them and make them feel wanted, because it's something I wanted very badly but never got.

One thing definitely hasn't changed since my rookie year. When I'm playing, I want to win more than anything else in the world. Maybe some players can hide that desire better than I can. Maybe it doesn't burn as brightly inside them. All I know is that I act the way I feel.

I've tried to be calm, cool, and collected like the other women. It doesn't work for me. I tried it seriously back in 1996, and had the worst stretch of my career.

Sure, I managed to stay in my seat and I looked perfectly under control, but I was miserable. I had stamped down my heart so far that I had smothered the fire inside me. The game was no fun anymore, because I wasn't allowing it to affect me. It was as if I had let someone suck out my personality and replace me with some zombie.

Finally, one of the women came over and said, "Where are you? Don't you want to win anymore?"

That helped me snap out of it. I realized that I had allowed my desire to keep my composure beat down my love for the game. Without that love and desire, I was just another player.

After that, I decided to be myself again. Now I react when I miss shots. You can see it in my face when I miss a shot I thought would be easy.

But I can do that because I am sure of one thing: I will never let any miss affect my next shot. If I am upset, fine. By the time I stride to the table for my next shot, it's history.

So I play with emotion. Forgive me. That does not make me a poor sport. On the contrary, I've always prided myself on preserving my integrity and maintaining the dignity of the game.

Because it doesn't matter if you're playing in a televised tournament or in a friend's basement. Pool is a social game, and it gives you infinite opportunities to show your friends and your opponents who you are and what you are made of. For me, there is no point in winning if you disgrace yourself or the game along the way.

That's especially important now, because we are trying to popularize and expand the sport of women's pool. Let's face it: pool's image used to be despicable. It was all about hustlers and drunks and speed junkies who would play all through the night in smoke-filled halls.

Now when people think of pool, they think of a sport the whole family can enjoy. The Women's Professional Billiard Association is a well-regarded organization with elegant players.

That is why we have a dress code: blouses and pants for all matches, semiformal wear for televised events. That is also why we are not allowed to drink at the tournament site or gamble when we are in town for tournaments.

So far, our work is paying off. We are on ESPN for nearly an hour every week, and a million people watch us, every time, no matter what else is on or at what hour we appear.

It is important to me that we keep the game growing this way. If you love the game, respect it. Don't spit on the floor of the poolroom or grab your crotch between shots. (I know both of these things work great for baseball, but somehow they just don't suit our sport.)

The most basic violation of pool etiquette is the attempt to distract your opponent while she is shooting. This is known as sharking.

Of course, it is very tempting to use any possible advantage you can. After all, you do want to win.

But ask yourself: Is this how I want to win? Because realistically, you could probably pocket a ball with your hand while your opponent isn't looking, if you really just want to win at any cost.

It seems to me more important to win with dignity. That is why I was so upset when players accused me of sharking when I first joined the tour. I think it may have been easier for them to claim that I was distracting them than to face the fact that I had ripped them up on the table.

If you want to avoid similar accusations, here are a few simple rules to follow.

Don't move, blink, or breathe while your opponent is shooting. Don't flip your hair, don't pour your drink, don't light your cigarette, and don't go into your old high school cheerleading routine when your opponent is about to shoot. For one thing, these tricks are old—everyone knows what you are up to, and you look cheap.

My theory is this: rather than trying to distract your opponent, step up to the plate. Meet the challenge. Practice, and improve your skills until you can win fair and square. It feels infinitely better.

I take a lot of pride in staying perfectly still when my opponent is shooting. It's not difficult, but it shows I've got class.

To tell the truth, when I'm shooting I could care less what someone else is doing. When I'm down on a shot, I'm focused. You could yell "Fire!" and I'd still go through my preshot routine. I cannot see anything but the balls on the table, and I'm not thinking of anything other than the target.

But most people are not like that. They get distracted by the music, by the people walking past, and by the firemen rushing in with their hoses blasting.

There is one situation, I'll admit, in which you'll catch me sharking. Shamelessly. That is during the pro-am charity events we hold the night before every tournament. I have played against celebrities like Paul Sorvino and Reggie Miller and have distracted them by whipping my hair in front of the pocket, standing seductively in front of the pocket, and moving side to side while they line up their shots. You've got to have a little fun once in a while.

The moment the tournament begins, it's a whole different story, because then I am determined to win on skill alone. If you come to a tour event, you will see the difference in my behavior when the shots count.

Etiquette is not just about sportsmanship. There are also issues of consideration. If you don't wear a glove and you use talcum powder to keep your hands smooth, use only a little, and never apply it over the table. That way, if it spills, it spills on the floor. Same goes for the chalk.

Never throw the chalk. If you throw it badly or your opponent does not catch it, she might end up with a blue streak on her clothes or her skin.

Chalk up before you shoot, not after. If you miss, it is your opponent's turn, and she will need the chalk. Plus, it sends a message to your opponent if you are chalking up before she shoots. You are saying, I know you are going to miss. It is fine to think this, but if you telegraph that impulse through your actions, you are going to be a very lonely player after a while.

Another easy way to make enemies is to offer a little friendly advice in the middle of a game. Even in practice, I never tell another player what he is doing wrong unless he asks. For one thing, it undermines his confidence. You are assuming that you know how to play better than he does.

If I am playing someone whom I am obviously better than, I will usually answer his questions when we are finished for the day. That way, he will know how to improve, but I won't undermine his game while he is playing.

Anyone looking for advice will ask. If they don't ask, don't tell.

Now for one of my pet peeves. Most poolrooms sell food and drinks. That is good, especially if you are playing fourteen, fifteen hours in a row, as I often do. This concession does not, however, grant you a license to plunk your soda and your greasy wings down on top of the table, or even on the rail.

Don't let the word *table* fool you. You wouldn't try to eat off an operating table, would you?

The reason I am so adamant about this is twofold. First, it is disrespectful to the sport. Second, it poses a real risk to the equipment. The slightest spill or grease stain can greatly affect the way the cloth plays. And stain remover won't fix it. A repairman has to come out, take the table apart, and recover it with new cloth, and that can cost a couple hundred dollars.

All these cases are pretty clear-cut. There is one issue, though that is a little murkier. Should you tell your opponent if she is about to shoot at the wrong ball?

This is not the same thing as admitting to a foul that you committed. That I do every time. You can foul by scratching (sinking the cue ball), pocketing the wrong ball, or hitting the cue ball so that after contact with the object ball no ball is pocketed and no ball touches a rail. This last foul is frequently missed by opponents, but I still say own up to it.

For some people, winning is everything and pool is just one arena in which to win. For me, it's the love of my life, and I don't want to cheat at it.

Now, what if an opponent is about to commit a foul? Do you save her the trouble—and cost yourself the ball in hand that might help you win the match? I'd say you're under no obligation to do that. She knows the rules; you didn't trick her. It's her own lapse in concentration. If she happens to be your grandmother who has raised you since your own parents ran away when you were three and she's having trouble breathing and every game could be her last, you might want to warn her. For your own peace of mind.

So let's say you've read this book carefully, you know how to play, you understand how not to act like a butthead, and you've earned your first tournament victory. Do you rub it in your opponent's face?

Nah. Just shake hands and wish him luck in his next match. Tell him he shot well, if he really did. Winning the match should give you enough satisfaction. If it doesn't, and you are the type of person who likes to pull the wings off butterflies, you might want to seek professional help.

In our tournaments, it is not just courtesy that keeps players from gloating, it's practicality. Our tournaments are double-elimination affairs, and even if you beat somebody once, you might see them again in the finals. It is not going to help you much if they are steaming mad and out for revenge.

FOCUS UNDER PRESSURE

Sometimes I wish pool were like boxing. At least then I could rely on instincts and reactions. See the punch coming, duck. See an opening, attack.

It's the same routine for a tennis player, or a hitter in baseball. See the ball and react. There is no time to think.

In pool, there is nothing but time. If you don't hit the ball, it's not going anywhere.

So there you are. Just you and the ball. It's like a first date, where nobody knows what to say to the other person, and you just sit there in that lingering, uncomfortable silence. Only this time, you know the pool ball is not going to make the first move.

It is all up to you.

And that makes for a pressure-filled situation. Think about it. In basketball, is there more pressure when bodies are flying and players are leaping into the lane looking to score or when one player stands alone at the free-throw line late in the game, with thousands of people watching?

In pool, every shot is a free throw. No one is standing in your way. Except yourself.

And that is the problem. Even in tournament play, you have thirty seconds at the table between each shot. Thirty seconds to think about everything that could go wrong. Is your arm moving smoothly? Are you standing correctly? What about your follow-through?

You've got thirty seconds to wonder whether this is the shot that will catapult you to victory or the one that will force you back into your seat to watch another player take home your trophy, your money, your glory.

It is a lot to think about.

But when you're on, you've got no worries. You trust your stroke and you know that the results will come. It's like a dance where you know the steps so well you can just let go and let the music's rhythm take over your body.

That state of mind is called being "in stroke," or "dead stroking." In other sports, it's known as being "in the zone."

The zone is a mighty fine place to be.

All you've got to do is look at the ball and move your arm without effort. Suddenly the ball is in the hole. Your eyes are choreographing their own ballet, and the table is your stage.

In the zone, you've got no doubts, no fears, never a second thought. It is more exhilarating than any drug could hope to be.

Every player, at every level, can enter the zone. It may not look identical for a beginner as it will for an advanced player, but the phenomenon is the same. Suddenly, for no explainable reason, you find yourself playing way above your head. You're so much better than you've ever been before. You might sink five or six balls in a row as a beginner, or run five racks as a more accomplished player. I have had many runs of over one hundred balls without a miss.

So be ready—these hot streaks are just as frequent for amateurs as they are for professionals. They come at every stage of the developmental process. You'll know you're on one if you're playing great and it feels effortless. The truth is that you put in a lot of effort just to get to this stage, but in that moment, you're gliding, not grinding.

Everyone says the zone is indescribable. I'm not so sure. I think it is intensely personal, though, so you have to find out what it means for you, what it feels like when you are in your zone.

If you treat it like a mystical happening, then your moments in the zone will be wonderful, and they may boost your confidence, but they will remain an unpredictable muse.

So the next time you emerge from the zone—and you do emerge, as if coming out from under hypnosis—analyze what happened internally. What did it feel like? What were you thinking about? Were you walking around the table differently? Moving around more or less than usual? The more clearly you can recall these elements, the better your chances are of returning to that state, or at least of duplicating its conditions, so that you are freed up to play your best.

When I'm in the zone, I stalk the table like a panther. My breath is deep and calm, and my tongue curls up against the roof of my mouth. When I get down to shoot, my eyes focus and my brow furrows in a way that would surely give me a headache if I tried to do it intentionally. Especially since I can stay that way for an hour and a half.

In the zone, I walk with confidence. There's nothing but cool air around me. All the eyes in the place are on me, from the moment I chalk up to the end of the follow-through on my stroke.

In the zone, I feel no pain. Which is saying something, because pain is part of my daily existence, due to the nerve damage from the metal rod in my spine that will have to be surgically replaced. I have postponed the surgery as long as possible, because I cannot imagine not being able to play pool for two years of rehabilitation. Besides that, I have bursitis in my shoulder, and rheumatoid arthritis in my joints.

Yet when I'm in dead stroke, I don't feel any of it. All my negative thoughts vanish.

I am left with sheer confidence. I make decisive shots, and every shot goes exactly where I want it to. I don't sense the cameraman five feet away and I don't hear the music and I don't see the people and I don't think about what I'm wearing or what if I scratch, and I don't wonder where my friends are sitting or whether my husband is around.

Only the shot exists.

When I miss a shot, I sit down and wait, and even waiting feels good then. I have this overwhelming clarity, and I don't mind waiting, because I know my opponent's going down. She can do whatever she wants with her turn and it's just not going to matter. I feel so much confidence when I'm in the zone that other people might not believe it, or they might mislabel it as cockiness or arrogance, but it is so real, and it is the greatest feeling I know.

Start thinking about your experiences in the zone, and try replicating the conditions that led you to enter into it. You cannot force yourself back into that state of mind at will, but you can prepare yourself for when it returns. Treat it like a guest who you want to come visit again. Make your body a willing host. Set the table just so and turn down the lights, and your guest may be more eager to return.

Even if you cannot get back to that elevated place, arranging your mind in that way will keep you from worrying about your arm, your stroke, and all those other nagging details that get between you and your ability to trust the shot you are about to take.

When you are on, you feel no pressure. But what about the rest of the time, when you feel you are not playing your best? Believe it or not, you will feel this way almost all the time. I do. It doesn't feel great, but it's not because you have an exaggerated sense of your own ability. It's just that you want to get better. If you are not in some way frustrated or dissatisfied with your performance, you will not improve.

This can be one of your greatest strengths and one of your most stubborn weaknesses. Even after you win a tournament, you might think about how you could have played better.

That attitude is good in a way, because it keeps you hungry. But you have to realize that no one is perfect, and therefore no one is a perfect pool player. That way, you can enjoy your accomplishments as they happen, instead of immediately looking for the next way to improve.

Everyone reacts differently when they feel they are playing poorly, but I can give you two words of advice: Don't panic. That seems pretty basic, but it is the only way to maintain control of your situation, which is the first step toward turning it around.

Don't turn on your game. I often hear people who miss a series of shots walk away from the table saying, "I suck." That's a good way to get yourself into a rut, but not a particularly good way of getting yourself out.

If I am playing poorly and I have missed a number of shots, I will adjust my game and play a little bit safer. Take easy shots, or play defensively, making your opponent shoot difficult shots. Don't get frustrated. Even if at that moment you can't outshoot your opponent, you can still outsmart him. Pretty soon, he'll be cursing himself, and you will have regained the upper hand.

Never start working on your stroke in the middle of a match. Trust me. Your stroke is there. It's been there. It did not abandon you, so don't abandon it. If you were lost at sea, would you throw away your rudder? If you were in the middle of a war, would you toss your best gun aside and pick up an untested one?

No. So relax. You're not going to be able to change your stroke during a match, and you don't have to, either. You are not going to improve on hours of practice with thirty seconds of adjustments in a pressure-packed situation. It just doesn't work. Dance with the partner you came with.

Do not get flustered, and do not let your opponent see that you are unnerved. If you saw someone moaning and crying at the table, would you be afraid of him? No. You would think he was ripe for the taking. So don't give your opponent that edge. Keep your composure.

The best way to do that is to sit calmly while your opponent shoots. Don't waste that time kicking yourself. Instead, talk to yourself. (Not out loud.) Think about how much you are looking forward to your next chance at the table. Tell yourself that you are warming up, that you're just getting going, and then when you do, there's going to be hell to pay.

That should end your streak of misery pretty quickly.

But what about those other times, when you are neither particularly hot nor particularly cold and you just happen to lose focus and miss a critical shot?

This happens to everyone. For me, one of the biggest challenges in the sport is to maintain discipline. I eat right, I work out, and I practice hard, so my long-term discipline is good, but there is another kind of in-the-moment discipline that I have had to struggle with.

That is the discipline to wait. To wait until my mind is perfectly focused on executing the shot flawlessly before I release. I have to remind myself to make sure that my mind is completely relaxed and at peace before I let my shot go.

Too often, I will shoot in a moment of indecision. I will be wondering whether I want to hit the ball on this side or that side, and for some reason, before I have figured it out, I will find myself shooting. You have probably experienced the same thing. And you've probably had the same results. The ball winds up somewhere between the two options, and the outcome is invariably ugly.

This leads to doubt, confusion, and a quick seat.

Instead, take a decisive shot. The decision you make does not matter as much as the fact that you made a decision.

When I am able to wait until I am dead certain of what I want to do, my accuracy is much, much better. I think that if you make up your mind, your body will follow. But if the mind is messed up, the body is much more likely to screw up the shot.

After many painful losses, I developed a way to make sure my mind is in the right place at the moment of truth. I have come to rely on my preshot routine.

MY PRESHOT ROUTINE

This routine is as important as anything else in this book.

You may think that as a recreational player you do not need a preshot routine, but I promise you that the quicker you incorporate it into your game, the quicker you will develop as a pool player.

The four-part preshot routine is the best way to maintain focus, no matter what conditions you face. It is your one assurance that you will be thinking about the shot in front of you when you shoot, instead of your next shot, the phone call you forgot to make, or that Internet stock you invested in last week.

Here it is.

First, make a decision about what you want to do. That is the easiest part, but it is important. Look for the best shot available, always keeping in mind that you want to establish cue-ball position for your next shot. I typically think an entire rack ahead, but that has come with years of playing. If you can think three shots ahead, you are doing fine. If two shots is your max, that's plenty, too. If you can only think about the shot right in front of you, you will run into trouble pretty quickly.

It helps to walk around the table, to get a lay of the land before deciding what shot looks the easiest or the most promising. This is a good time to chalk up. A new perspective can change your thinking in a hurry, and that might make the difference between winning and losing a close match.

All right, you've made your decision.

Next, picture the shot happening exactly as you intend it. Picture it in as much detail as you can. Visualize the speed of the cue ball and its entire path around the table, from start to finish. Picture it going exactly where you want it to go, watch it hit the object ball, and watch that object ball go whisking into the pocket.

The more detailed your visualization, the more your body will make it happen, and the more accurate you will be, especially in terms of speed control and the cue ball's reaction off the object ball. Trust your brain. If it won't imagine something happening, it could be a sign that what you want to do is not possible. Your brain knows physics, even if you failed it in high school. It has incorporated all the knowledge it has gathered from seeing bodies in motion all these years—believe that it knows what it's talking about.

Negative visualizations are powerful, too. If you keep seeing the cue ball scratch, you will make it happen. Don't take a shot where you see an unhappy ending looming. Go back to the beginning of the routine, and make a new decision.

The third step in the preshot routine involves your aim. Get down on the shot, and find your smallest possible target. Look at the cue ball, the object ball, and your pocket. Then focus on the object ball, and find that one atom-sized dot, the tiniest place in the universe that you can imagine. Narrow your vision. The fact is, the more precise your aim, the more accurate you will be. Period.

Aim is just as much about your mind as your eyes. People tend to say after a miss, "Oh, I was thinking about this" or "I was looking at that lady in the stands."

Your mind is almost never completely blank; therefore, it has to be thinking of something when you shoot. Let that thought be all about making your shot and focusing on the smallest possible target. Concentrate on making that the thought. Don't just hope that perfect aim happens to be your thought, because it probably won't be, unless you make it your last thought.

If you are thinking about anything else, your focus is not where it should be at that moment—on the table.

The final step may be the hardest. You have to trust yourself and let your stroke go. Just let it go. Take your practice strokes and say, "I know this ball's going in."

If you have any doubts, do not take the shot.

Get up and start from step one again. Seriously.

You cannot question yourself once you are down on the shot. If you do, you absolutely must get back up and go through the whole process all over again. If you have decided to hit that ball high right, hard, with a follow motion and at the last second you see trouble, don't try to adjust on the spot. Stand up, breathe, and think everything through again. If you are on the clock, ask for a fifteen-second extension. If you try to change your shot while you are down on it, you will not see the entire table, you will shoot hastily, and you will kick yourself later for having shot during a moment of indecision.

WINNING AND LOSING ATTITUDES

There must be fifteen to twenty women on the professional tour who have as much skill as I do. They can match me shot for shot, ball for ball.

Yet they don't win tournaments. Sometimes they get ahead a couple of games, but they can't close the deal. Other times they fall behind, and they can't get up and fight back. These players are always lurking in the top ten or twenty, but they never find their way into the winner's circle.

Then, of course, there are the champions. Women who come through time after time. Women who never give up, who never let their opponent walk out of a dangerous corner. Women with the killer instinct of a black widow.

The difference between these groups isn't luck or magic fingers. It's all in their attitudes.

Seeing people exhibit winning and losing attitudes can be the most fascinating and informative part of watching a pool tournament.

You can tell a winner from a loser by the way they react in difficult situations. The most obvious scenario comes up when a player is faced with an extremely difficult shot. These shots are considered "out of line," because there is no direct route for the object ball to reach the pocket.

Put yourself at the table. You're cruising along. One ball, two, now three. You sink the third, but that darned cue ball suddenly shows a mind of its own, darting and dancing into areas you didn't

A fighter's mentality: Sometimes the difference between winning and losing is all in your mind.

want it to go. You check out the table, and there's no doubt about it—you're out of line.

What now? Do you curse yourself? Start the recriminations? Tell yourself that you just can't bring it when the pressure is on?

I don't. I look over at my opponent, who is usually half out of her seat, looking for the chalk and planning her next assault. "Oh, she's not going to like this," I say to myself.

Because I know I'm going to deliver that shot, and I'm going to make her slump in her chair and drop her designer cue. I know for a fact that I'm going to get out of trouble.

At no point do I say, "Darn, I'm not going to win now."

I don't pity myself. Because there is no time for self-pity. I've got a shot to make.

It's all about meeting the challenge. Because life does not just line up for you to conquer it. If it were that easy, we wouldn't need eighty years to get it right.

Sometimes the attitudes become clear before the games even begin. I remember that when I was an amateur, professionals would occasionally sign up for a spot in our local tournaments. As soon as word got out, almost everybody bitched and moaned about how this pro was going to take all our money and run.

I wanted to see her try.

Not because I was cocky enough to think she couldn't beat me. Of course she could. But to me, that just made the matchup more exciting.

Because the only way to get better is to play people better than you.

You may not win. But you will get stronger, and you will learn what it takes to be a winner. To me, that's the essence of competition: pushing your limits, testing yourself against the best. That is the best way to improve, and the only way to become a champion.

If you don't have that attitude, you might as well pack your bags. Even if you win the tournament against watered-down competition, you are never going to get anywhere in life ducking challenge after challenge.

A lot of people say that the difference between winning and losing comes down to which player wants it more.

I think you can want it pretty badly and still lose. There is a difference between desire and motivation: it is easy to want something; what is hard is translating that desire into action.

When I was a young player coming up, I wanted to be number one so badly I could feel it boiling in my blood. It was the first thing I thought of in the morning, and the last before I went to bed.

But it didn't happen just because I wanted it to. I used that desire to motivate me. It became the force that woke me up every morning. It whipped me to get to the poolroom an hour before my friends, so I could practice before we played.

And I allowed it to shape my dreams.

I never sat there and said, "I'm going to go on tour this year, and I hope I do well." Or, "I'm just going to go in there and do my best."

That sounds nice but, to me, it's a recipe for failure. I say set a real goal and go for it.

Don't be afraid of setting your goals too high. I'd be afraid of setting them too low. One of the women on the tour came up to me crying last year after a tournament in New York. She had come in tenth for the fifth time in six tournaments. She is a talented player, as good a shot maker as we have on the tour, but she couldn't get over the hump.

"What did you set out to do at the beginning of the year?" I asked her.

"I wanted to finish in ninth through twelfth place as often as I could," she said.

Mission accomplished. Goal met. And there she was, crying.

So set your goals high, and do what it takes to meet them. Desire without action is a waste. You've got to let your hunger lead you somewhere.

The way to do that is to show your commitment to the sport today. Not someday. Today. Go to the poolroom. You know that shot you always miss? Set it up, and knock it down. One hundred times. Two hundred. Three hundred. As many times as it takes you to master it. And suddenly, you'll see that one of your glaring weaknesses has been transformed into a strength. You put in some time, and now you are a better player, with one more bullet in your gun.

How's that feel?

It is important to enjoy every small step of your improvement, especially once you have set lofty goals. Otherwise it is easy to become discouraged. What if you don't become number one in six months? What if you still can't beat the town ace after twenty weeks of practice?

Doesn't matter.

Beginners get all wrapped up in results. Forget about results. They will come. You will meet your goal when you stop bludgeoning yourself for your failure to meet it.

It's a journey, just like everything else in life. Everybody wants a shortcut. That's why we have so many systems for aiming—everybody wants the quick road to success.

But I have learned something: I'm never going to reach my goal. I will always want to play better. And this game is so challenging (and so frustrating) that I will never play the perfect game I want to play. The more I know, the more I see how much I still have to learn.

Set a goal, but savor every improvement along the way. Many people will try to break you down, so you've got to be able to pat yourself on the back and celebrate your achievements. Because it feels great to achieve things.

It won't feel great in the traditional sense; it's more like going to the gym. I mean, why does that feel good? You grunt and groan and sweat and work your muscles through exhaustion and agony. But you feel good about it, because you know you have done something positive for yourself. It sounds so simple, but there is an enormous difference between going to sleep proud of yourself and slinking off to sleep filled with shame.

Taking stock of that process will make your life infinitely richer. Go to bed every night knowing that you've enriched your life just a little bit more. Think about what you've done that day. Have you done what you set out to do?

Whether you have or you haven't, there is another question that is just as important: What are you going to do tomorrow?

I always find myself wondering, "How can I improve as a person?"

I never walk around thinking I'm perfect, either as a player or as a person. I am always trying to improve—my game, my health, everything. To me, everything is integrated, and if I can become a better person, I know it will come out on the table. I am never going to stop trying to better myself. I want to learn to speak more eloquently, to improve my education, my marketing skills, my public relations, and my relationships with my friends.

Not that I'm out there looking for more friends. I have a lot already. And while you can never have too many friends, I have realized that friends are not something you can just make overnight. You have to earn and develop your friendships.

I'm always thinking about what I can do for my friends. I try to come up with new ways to be generous, and kind.

But sometimes I feel terrible just the same, because I wonder if I'm just doing it to conquer that part of myself that feels so selfish and unkind. It seems like I can't win, but I'll go on trying just the same.

Having this willingness to face your fears and keep on learning about yourself and your limitations is key to becoming both a better player and a better person.

So let this hunger for self-knowledge work for you. Study yourself honestly, both your personality and your game. Admit your strengths and face your weaknesses. This attitude will take you further than any fancy cue stick.

And it doesn't matter if you're the last-place finisher in your local tournament or the top-ranked player on the professional tour. For all of us, I think, life is a kind of mission: to continue to grow and learn all the things we need to know to get better.

This attitude can make the difference between a player who grows and develops and one who stagnates and never changes.

Plenty of players practice, practice, practice but still don't improve that much. I analyze my game the same way I analyze myself. I try to be a student of the game, so that I can make the most out of my practice time. I think about what is missing from my game and figure out what I need to do to fine-tune every aspect of my playing.

My goal is to take what I have and transform it into a package that is utterly unstoppable, invincible, and invulnerable, so that nobody in the world can beat me.

No matter how well you play, you should still maintain this outlook of a student, because there is always more to learn—the table provides a nearly infinite number of combinations to master.

Of course, there is a time and a place for this student role. Take this role only during practice. You don't want to be a student when you're competing, because when you're competing, it's war. You give up any chance you have of winning if you sit there marveling at your opponent and philosophizing in the middle of battle.

Kill first, study later. That's the attitude you need to have if you want to win big in this sport.

And while you're killing, never complain about the equipment. That's a loser move, and a sure sign of a faulty attitude. Professionals do it all the time.

"Isn't this cloth a little fast?" they'll ask.

"I love this cloth," I'll tell them.

"Aren't the pockets kind of thin?" they want to know.

"The pockets are perfect," I respond.

Truth is, I love whatever I am playing on. Because whether I love it or not, I'm playing on it. We all are. And the first player who stops fighting the inevitable and learns to embrace it has the best chance to win.

It's not that I don't recognize when conditions are different from what I'm used to. I just accept the challenge. I know that if I had played my whole life on that cloth, with those pockets, it would be no problem. It's just a question of adjusting, and I can do it in an instant, because I know it can only help me. What good does it do to complain? Will the cloth get slower? Will the pockets expand? I don't think so.

Same goes for the layout of the room. If your opponent hits a shot that leaves you in a tight spot near the wall, where you have to use the shorty cue, don't roll your eyes or complain. Grab that shorty cue off the rack with a smile. Make your shot, and at the next available opportunity leave the cue ball by the rail, in such a way that he has to use the shorty cue. Watch him wriggle and squirm, and know that you have got him mentally beat already.

15 LEARN FROM LOSING

A wise woman once told me that the key determinant of success is the way you handle failure. And it's true. No one climbs the mountain in one smooth ascent. There are always pitfalls and pratfalls, accidents along the way. That's probably the toughest lesson to learn in life, and one of the most important.

If you believe that everything is always going to go your way, you're not going to be prepared when something goes wrong. And believe me, something will go wrong.

When it does, what will your reaction be? When you're knocked down, will you be able to get up off the canvas? Because that is when champions are made. Not in the champagne celebrations or the victory parades, but in the moments when competition is fierce, when victory seems miles away and defeat is imminent.

I have been down that road.

In 1993, my rookie year, I made a series of good showings. I came in third in one tournament and fourth in the next, but I had never made it to the finals in any tournament.

Then came the World Championships, which were held that year in Königswinter, Germany. The best of the best gathered to battle for the most prestigious title in the sport.

And when the tournament began, I was hot. I tore through the competition. At that time, I didn't know the intricacies of the game at all. I didn't have much cue-ball control, and I didn't plan two shots in advance. I had two things going for me: I could sink a ball from anywhere, and I knew it.

The confidence was just as much a part of my success as my shot-making ability. But it also proved to be part of my downfall. The other women on tour resented both my achievements and my attitude. They thought that because I was a rookie, I hadn't paid my dues.

It didn't matter that I had practiced thousands of hours alone in the poolroom, or that I played straight pool matches to one thousand points when the other women typically stopped at one hundred. To them, I was a novice, a beginner, an upstart.

And they let me know it.

As I advanced through the World Championship tournament, they began to boo me. Every time I stepped up to the table, I heard catcalls and taunts from other American players. It didn't matter who I was playing, or where they were from. The women that I had played with all year rooted for my opponents, even when they were from countries halfway round the world. Some international players had a field day questioning the American players' patriotism.

I managed to block out the distractions and keep winning until I reached the finals against Loree Jon Jones, a legend of the game. At that point, it got out of control.

The finals were played under a special format. We were to play the best two out of three sets. Each set was over when one player won seven games.

In the first set, I heard the boos. In fact, I heard little else. I couldn't concentrate. Not surprisingly, Loree Jon beat me in a close set. The girls were getting what they wanted. I was playing scared.

After the set, I headed for the bathroom. There I took a moment to compose myself. I realized that I was making it too easy for the people rooting against me. I decided that if this woman was going to beat me, she was going to have to beat me playing my best. There was no way I was just going to hand it to her.

And I went out and blitzed her. The second set was all mine.

As the third set started, the roar of the crowd grew even more intense. It was as if they were rising up as one to crush me. And instead of bearing down like an experienced player would have, I panicked.

It wasn't just the crowd, though. There was something else going on. I had realized the significance of the situation, and had seen how close I was to success. And I had been awed. Remember, I was a twenty-three-year-old rookie who had never won a tournament in my own country, playing on a continent I had never visited, with a chance to be the champion of the world. Truth is, I wasn't ready.

I had found a way to overcome adversity, but now that I was staring success in the face, I blinked. It is paradoxical, but it is amazing how powerful the fear of success can be. I dropped that third set.

It was just too much for me to take right then. I'd been swinging on an emotional pendulum, and I couldn't find my balance. And so I lost.

But everybody loses. It happens. Michael Jordan didn't win a championship as a rookie either. It just doesn't work that way. You have to lose before you can win. Sorry. It's painful to lose. It feels worse than anything else in the world to watch your opponent leaping up and down, to hear the crowd go crazy for someone else. You are the sacrificial lamb, the beaten and bloody gladiator. But you are a necessary part of the ritual, the spectacle of sport.

Once you accept that, the question then becomes, How do you get to the other side of the table? How do you become the exultant champion, the hero, the one riding the audience's cheers?

You do that by learning from your loss.

You have to figure out what happened. Don't ignore the wound and hope it closes by itself. If you do, you'll be left with a terrible scar. Use your pain as motivation—not just to get angry, but to do something about it.

I have thought for the last ten years about what happened that night in Königswinter. The memory drives me to this day—it makes my quest for the world title one of the most important things in my life.

But it is not just a festering sore. It has become a launching pad for me. I figured out my technical mistakes, and also my mental ones: my lapses in concentration, my listening to the crowd.

I learned that to succeed, you have to prepare your mind at least as thoroughly as you prepare your body.

And so I did. I developed the techniques encompassed in this book. And after that, I started winning. At the next tournament, in Baltimore, I won. The women still didn't accept me. After the victory, I went into a seafood restaurant where they were all feasting on crab cakes and lobsters.

No one even looked up.

No one said hi, or congratulated me on my first win. I sat in the corner, ate my crab legs, and walked back to my hotel room alone. I cried myself to sleep.

It took me a while to heal, but eventually I learned my lesson. I had wanted so badly to be their friend. I had felt so tortured and worried so much about how these people saw me, without ever realizing how I saw them.

Once I stopped focusing on trying to get them to like me, their opinion didn't seem so powerful anymore. For almost a year, I had swallowed their vision of who I was, and by now it was making me sick.

Instead of trying to get them to like me, or acting like the bad girl they thought I was, I decided just to be true to myself and let the chips fall where they may. There was no way they were going to intimidate me anymore.

I won the next tournament, and the one after that, and by the end of that year I was the number one ranked professional in the world.

And it wouldn't have happened without that loss in Germany.

Now let's be realistic. I would rather win than lose. I would rather sail into a tournament finals undefeated, because then I have total confidence. I feel more at ease, more comfortable playing my game.

But I always learn more from my losses that I do from my wins. Every time I lose, I see another weakness, another chink in my armor. And that spurs me to go forward and fix it. To transform a weakness into a strength.

Losing has also taught me graciousness. So many people lose and then say, "I can't believe how lucky she got!"

Or they'll say, "She never would have beat me if I was playing well."

That's a sore loser, and a sure sign of someone who has let bitterness poison their view of the world.

Let's face it: no matter how lucky the other person got, to win a tournament match she had to clear the table nine times!

I have never in my life had someone break and run out nine racks on me. It just doesn't happen. Which means that in every match I have played, I have had a chance to step up to the table and take a shot.

At some point then, I had control of the table, and I let it go. My opponent never would have had the chance to get lucky if I had taken care of business.

I just hate to put all the blame and all the responsibility on someone, or something, other than myself. That's saying, "I had no control over the situation."

And not only is that not true, it is more intolerable to me than thinking that my opponent got lucky. Because if you have no control, you're helpless. You can't make a difference, and you can't change your fate.

If, on the other hand, you take responsibility for what happened at the table, if you fess up to your actions and your mistakes, then you can make a difference the next time.

I'm not going to say that luck is never involved in pool. Of course I have lost some treacherous matches, where I have shot atrociously, or my opponent has had a good run of luck.

That's when I smile, shake my opponent's hand, and wish her luck in the next match.

Maybe it's just my ego, but I'm convinced that any opponent must have played pretty well to beat me, no matter what the circumstances. I am as good a player as there is on earth, and as dedicated to my sport, and I've got to believe that no one is going to beat me playing badly.

And since our tournaments are double-elimination affairs, I usually walk away hoping that I meet that person again, down the road in the finals.

PRACTICE FOR PERFORMANCE

A lot of players spend hours banging balls around the table, joking and drinking with friends while the music is blasting. Then later they wonder, "How come I'm not improving?"

It's like a painter who sits around throwing paint at a canvas for a year and wonders why his portraits don't get any better. It's true they put the time in, but it's not the right kind of time.

To actually improve as a pool player, you should engage in two kinds of practices: analytical practice and competitive practice.

Analytical practice is the time you give yourself to learn and grow as a player and a student of the game. Play against someone who is better than you. Warm up by shooting fairly easy shots, con-

Perfect practice makes for perfect pool.

necting with the cue ball at twelve and six o'clock on the ball face.

These shots provide a sure way to gauge your improvement. Are you making more of them than you did last month? Last week? Last night? Plus, when you miss one of these simple shots, it is easy to tell what you did wrong. You can change it immediately, so you don't continue making the same errors and enforcing bad habits. On complex shots, there are many more variables, and it is sometimes difficult to pinpoint which factor made you miss.

Easy shots also help boost your confidence and put you in the right frame of mind for practice. This warm-up routine is no different from the layup drills that basketball teams do before a game.

Don't try English or massé shots right away. They will mess with your stroke and your confidence. You don't see hoopsters trying desperation three-pointers before the game, do you?

Next, do some drills. Practice your break. Developing a solid break that frequently pockets balls is essential to victory, because it gives you initial control of the table. You want that.

Practice speed control. You can do that by visualizing exactly the speed you will need to make the cue ball travel twice across the table so that it touches two rails. Notice how far off your visualization is and adjust. Soon it won't be off at all.

Now practice your cut shots. If one particular angle gives you trouble, line it up and knock it down twenty, fifty, one hundred times. Make light chalk marks on the table (just twisting the overturned chalk once will do the trick) where you want to line up the cue ball and object ball, so you can ensure that you are actually shooting the same shot each time.

That is how I got better; I was as devoted to drills as I was committed to competition.

Once your drills are out of the way, start a game of nine-ball. This is still analytical practice, so don't worry about being interrupted. You can smoke cigarettes, flirt with the babes at the next table—whatever you need to do to make this practice time enjoyable. If you're at the poolroom as much as I am, you can even take your phone calls there during this time (don't tell the guy from Amsterdam Billiards I told you that—he's not too fond of playing secretary). Just make sure you're focused when you're at the table.

Feel free to ask your opponent questions about how he made a particular shot. Really enjoy this time, and use it to learn all you can about the sport. It is a great opportunity to absorb the atmosphere and the ambience of the room while learning the intricacies of the game. Your overall game will improve quickly, and your love for pool will continue to grow.

Unfortunately, analytical practice isn't enough to help you take home tournament checks. For that, you have to engage in what I call competitive practice.

In competitive practice, you want everything to be just the way it is during your tournaments. Most people, including some professionals, ignore this second kind of practice, and it puts them at a distinct disadvantage once the pressure is on and the TV cameras are staring them in the face. They're just not ready, or they're not comfortable enough in pressure situations to perform well.

So prepare yourself in advance. That is the goal of competitive practice.

Pick a table that is the same size as the ones used for your tournament. Make sure it is covered in the same speed cloth. Turn down the music and play with intensity, just the way you would in a tournament.

Be sure to pick a partner who is also looking for competitive practice, or you will both want to kill each other before the day is done. You are allowed just one five-minute break during this session, so do whatever you have to do before your start. Smoke your butts, buy your drinks, and clean out your system. If you are a regular at the poolroom, ask the manager to hold your calls, and turn off your cell phone.

It's time for business.

Play nine-ball, and race to nine games. Play by tournament rules: the first player to take nine games wins. Instead of flipping a coin to see who breaks, lag for it.

Maintain complete silence throughout the session.

Wear exactly what you would wear during a tournament. If you practice every day in sweats and then bust out a suit come tournament time, you are not going to be comfortable, and you are not going to play well. So play in the suit a few times. The other option—wearing your sweats to the tournament—is really not as appealing.

Setting up all these elements may seem contrived, and it may feel like a pain the first few times you do it. But there is really no better way to prepare your mind for the rigors of competition. The more comfortable you are with the formality, the more accustomed you are to the pressure-cooker atmosphere of a tournament, the more you will be able to play your game with a smooth stroke, a clear head, and a steady eye.

To me, tournaments are wars. Consider competitive practice your basic training. You wouldn't want to walk straight from the beach onto a battlefield, would you? You need to be prepared.

To win at pool you need a cut-throat attitude. This may sound unladylike, but when you are competing you should be thinking about how badly you want to rip out your opponent's throat. To do so without getting arrested is to play the best pool you can play. Keep her pinned to her seat. Give her no air to breathe.

You don't want an ounce of doubt or fear or confusion lurking in your body during tournament play or competitive practice. It is all about confidence. If you make an error and give your opponent a chance to shoot, fine. She got lucky. It won't happen again.

And while you're sitting on that chair, waiting for your turn, you're planning to destroy your opponent. It's you or her. No questions, none at all. Do or die. Who'll draw first blood? If you want it to be you, use the following practice drills.

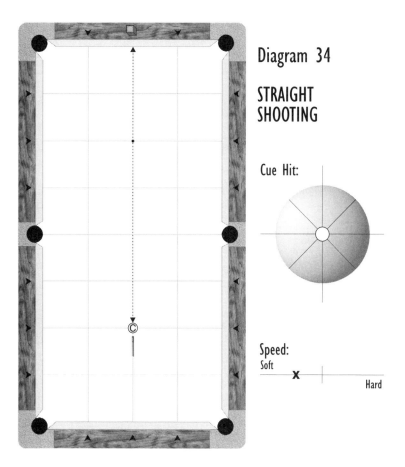

Diagram 34

STRAIGHT SHOOTING

Cue Hit:

Speed:
Soft

X

Hard

This basic drill will show you just how accurate your stroke is. Place the cue ball on the head spot, aim straight down toward the opposite diamond, and stroke softly at the center of the cue ball. You want the cue ball to strike the far rail and rebound right back to the middle of your cue tip. If the ball comes back to your left, you are accidentally using left English, and if the ball comes back to your right, you are accidentally using right English. The farther your shot returns in either direction, the farther from dead-center you are stroking the cue ball. Practice until you get it right, then try the same drill with different speeds.

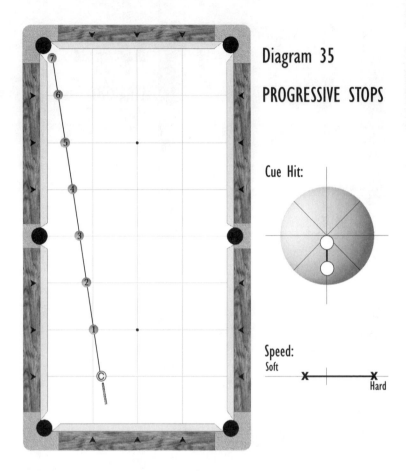

Diagram 35

PROGRESSIVE STOPS

Cue Hit:

Speed:
Soft

Hard

Try to sink the object ball and get the cue ball to stop on contact. On your first shot, place the object ball on the spot closest to the cue ball; then move it progressively farther away each time. As the distance increases, use more speed and strike the cue ball lower.

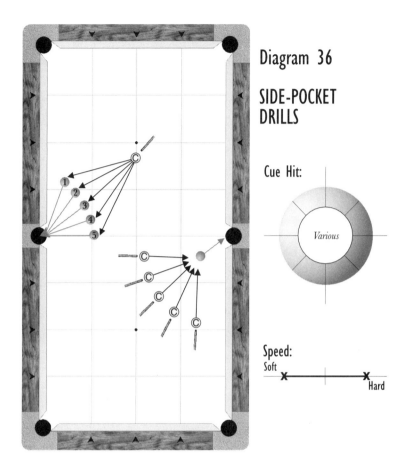

Diagram 36

SIDE-POCKET DRILLS

Cue Hit:

Various

Speed:
Soft ✗ ————————— ✗
Hard

Set up the 1- through 5-balls in a rainbow near the side pocket. After each shot, return the cue ball to its original position. Then go to the opposite side pocket, but this time keep the object ball in one place and move the cue ball in an arc, changing the angle for each shot. Side-pocket shots are both difficult and important, and this drill will give you a leg up on your opponents.

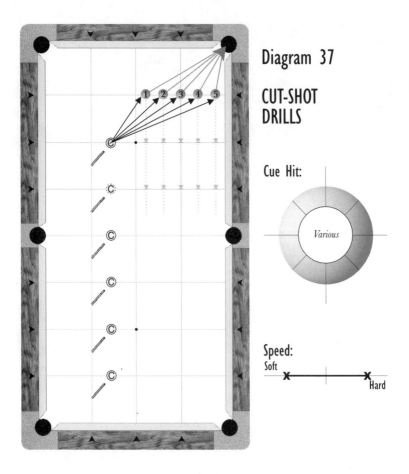

Diagram 37

CUT-SHOT DRILLS

Cue Hit:

Various

Speed:

Soft ✗————————✗ Hard

Line up the 1- through 5-balls near the pocket. Shoot at each ball, but after each shot return the cue ball to its original position. Once you master these angles, move both the object balls and the cue balls one diamond down the table, farther from the pocket. To make the drill even more challenging, move the cue ball progressively farther down the table. Keep track of your progress, and you'll soon see cut shots becoming much, much easier.

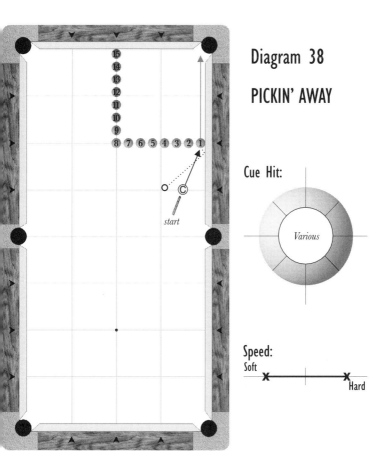

Diagram 38

PICKIN' AWAY

Cue Hit:

Various

Speed:
Soft ✗ ✗ Hard

This is a difficult drill that will challenge any player, no matter how talented. Line up all fifteen balls as shown. Start with the cue ball in hand and try to run as many balls in numerical order as possible, without touching any other balls and without ever picking up the cue ball. This will test your accuracy and your ability to play into position for your next shot.

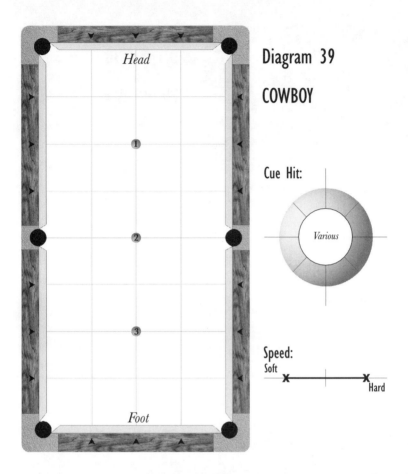

Diagram 39

COWBOY

Cue Hit:

Various

Speed:
Soft ✗————————✗ Hard

This may be the best drill for players at all levels to improve their position play. Set up the 1-, 2-, and 3-balls as shown. The object is to pocket one of the three object balls and then have your cue ball carom into one of the other two. After you make a ball, put it back on its designated spot. If you do not pocket the ball, leave it where it stops and try again. If you're playing Cowboy against an opponent, your turn ends when you fail to sink a ball and carom into another ball. Each ball is worth its face value when it gets sunk and caromed into by the cue ball on a made shot. For example, if you sink the 1 and hit the 3, that's four points. Play to seventy-five.

THE HUSTLE

Hustling. It's always the first thing reporters want to ask me about, and the last thing I want to discuss.

The truth is, every female professional player has worked hard to shed the image of the hustler. Because what woman wants to be known as a hustler?

To me, a hustler is a cheater and a liar, a parasite and a bully. Hustlers will shoot badly, dupe unsuspecting people into playing them for money, and then miraculously improve as soon as the big money is on the line.

Up until the 1990s, the hustler was the dominant image of our sport.

I hope that now when people think of pool, they typically think of beautiful women in elegant clothes, showing off their talents in front of a worldwide audience.

It's quite a difference, and it hasn't happened by accident. The women of the Women's Professional Billiard Association have made it happen by carefully cultivating a classy image.

As I mentioned before, we have a strict dress code—although I have been known to break it now and again with outfits they find to be too sexy. Our most important rule, however, is no gambling in the cities where we are playing. It just makes sense. You don't go into a town to sell your product and rip off the townsfolk while you're there. It's selfish and shortsighted.

But I'm not going to lie to you and say I never gambled. Please. I gambled all the time when I was coming up.

It was just about the only money I could count on, since it's pretty hard to keep other jobs when you're playing pool all the time.

Still, I never really considered myself a hustler. I just took advantage of men who behaved like stupid orangutans looking to take my money.

See, I never once pretended that I was a worse player than I actually was. I never purposely missed shots to give my opponent false confidence. I consider that lying, and I could not live with myself if I wasn't true to myself and to the sport I love.

These men, though, couldn't care less how well I shot in warm-ups. To them, I was "just a woman." They would offer to play me, then give me ridiculous handicaps that I really didn't need.

It happened all the time. Almost every day I'd hear, "Hey baby, let me show you how to really shoot some stick."

Most of the time I didn't have enough money to challenge these guys. Luckily, there were a couple guys I knew pretty well at the poolroom, and one of them would always offer to be my stakehorse: they put up the cash so that after the match, they could take home part of my winnings.

Back then, I really did need the money I won—I had no other consistent income, and some mornings I woke up without a penny in my pocket. When you know that you either win or go hungry, you tend to win a lot.

Desperate as I was for the money, it gradually became a secondary priority for me. I liked taking down these guys' egos. It never failed—by the end of the match, a crowd would have gathered, poking fun and pointing at the big shot who was somehow losing to a girl.

So yes, gambling is frowned upon, and in some places it's illegal. But I can't say it isn't fun.

There is actually a real benefit to playing someone for money. It puts you in a pressure situation, because you really have put something on the line. This is the way to play if you want to become a true competitor—with the adrenaline coursing through you so fast that your stomach is in knots and you can't take in enough oxygen and you feel like you're on the verge of either hiding in the closet or peeing in your pants.

This pressure works in two ways. First, it can cause you to get nervous and choke. You might miss easy shots that you would make ten times in a row in practice. Yet there is a second effect that pressure can have, and this is the one you need to harness to become the player to beat: with higher stakes, you focus more and take the time to make good, firm decisions.

Nowadays, though, you can get the benefit of playing under pressure without gambling. You can play your friends in a pool league to add the element of competition without sacrificing the friendly, social aspects of the game. Or you can join one of the many local tournaments in your area. The financial risk is far smaller than gambling—just an entry fee—but the potential winnings are pretty nice.

I don't gamble anymore. I don't want to set a bad example and I don't need to gamble to improve my game. I get a bigger adrenaline rush playing in front of a million people with my world ranking on the line than I do in a back room playing for a pile of twenties. Even an extremely large pile.

The last time I gambled was in a real serious hall on the outskirts of Bellflower, California, back in 1995. I had agreed to play with a partner against two other guys for a total pot of $100,000.

The rule was winner-take-all, no quitting till the game was done. We went up $75,000, and had $25,000 more to go. By this time, though, we'd been playing about twenty-three hours straight, and I was feeling it. I could barely keep my eyes open.

Meanwhile, these guys kept retreating to the bathroom, and every time they came out, they were like jumping beans, racing around the table, raring to go. I didn't know if they were taking speed or what, but I knew I wasn't about to give away all that money

I'd earned to a couple of junkies just because they could stay awake on drugs.

I was about to break down, and the whole scene was getting ugly. The guy I was playing with was starting to miss every shot, and our opponents were getting hot. They won two sets at twenty grand apiece. I needed a nap, but they wouldn't give me even half an hour, because they knew they would come crashing down. Lucky for me, just as I was feeling desperate to get out of the game, another great player came through the doors, looking for some action.

We "put him in the box," which means he joined the game, taking my place. My partner and I split what we had won, and the four of them kept on playing while I walked out the door.

When I woke up the next morning, I knew I didn't want to do it anymore. I had been gambling nonstop for almost six months. I had entirely changed my whole daily schedule, sleeping till three in the afternoon so I would be fresh when the money games came around. I had stopped caring about the tournaments, and even the game itself.

It had become all about the action. That morning, I saw how much I had changed. It was an ugly world, ruled by greed. I had to bark at people all the time, trying to intimidate, insult, or rile them up enough to where they were dying to play me for money. I couldn't trust anybody. I was acting like someone I would never want to hang around with, much less be.

After that twenty-three-hour marathon, I snapped out of it. I realized that I didn't need that life. I have sponsors, I have tournaments—I can make my money legitimately. That way, I never have to worry about the people who leave the poolroom and have to go home and do some serious explaining or, even worse, the people who leave so broke that they cannot even get home. It's happened.

Looking back, I really hope I never took anyone's paycheck over the pool table. I'd hate to think of the angry wife, the starving kid with no milk in the bottle. You just never know.

My husband, George Breedlove, isn't quite as squeamish about his hustling past. George is a former pro on the men's tour, and he didn't just gamble like I did—he had a whole hustler's routine.

He'd cruise into some dusty town and check into a fleabag motel. He'd put on a painter's outfit and hit the hardware store for a can of paint. Back in his room, he'd splatter paint all over himself and dunk his hands in the can of latex. Then he'd wash his hands so that the paint just clung to his cuticles. The devil is always in the details.

Once he had established his disguise, he'd sidle into a rundown poolroom and pick up a game for three or four dollars.

He'd lose at first, missing all kinds of shots while his opponent decided that George was an easy mark. He'd know better, though, by the end of the night, when George would walk out the door with a couple grand in his pocket. Sometimes, walking out wasn't so easy—one time he won a few grand too many at a hall in southern Indiana and only made it out alive because his friend was carrying a .22-caliber pistol.

Times have changed, and George has changed his ways. Truth is, there aren't many guys doing the hustler routine anymore, and I really wouldn't worry about getting shaken down. Hustling is a lost art. Once the movies *The Hustler* and *The Color of Money* came out, everybody knew the tricks, and basically that was that.

Still, it pays to be careful. Don't gamble with anyone you don't know, and don't let the stakes rise beyond your means. If you're in a game with strangers, look around and try to figure out who the sucker is. If you don't see one, it's probably you.

Somebody who has been playing in a room for a few months probably isn't a hustler. The only reason a hustler would stick around for months is to find a big fish playing a high-stakes game. If that's you, be extra careful. And don't trust anybody in a painter's uniform.

LIFE ON TOUR

18 JOINING THE TOUR

Getting to the tour is far from an impossible dream. It is a process. If you have read this book, studied it, put in the time at the table, and made the most of your skills, you will probably have had the chance to play in some local amateur tournaments.

If you think you are good enough to play in these tournaments but haven't heard about them, ask at your local poolroom. The best halls always have up-to-date information, and many of them run leagues that will help you test your mettle.

Clearly, not everyone reading this book is looking to join the professional tour. But the lessons I learned, coming up through the ranks from the amateurs to the qualifying events to the heights of the pro tour, can help make anyone a better player.

I started out just like every other pool-hall player looking to reach the big time. Every time I heard about a tournament, I would scrape up the cash and enter—even if it meant a three-hour train ride and a cramped weekend in a motel room with five or six friends.

Part of me still misses those days. Everything seemed so simple, because it was all about pool. No endorsements, no autographs, no TV cameras, and no interviews. On the other hand, there was no money, no interest, and no glamour. So you take the good with the bad. Tournaments are still the only way I know for an amateur to become a better player.

It's kind of like the bush leagues for a baseball player. You might wait down there forever, or you might get called up to the show. You never know. The only thing you can be sure of is that if you don't play in these tournaments, you will never be staring me down in a finals match on ESPN.

That is because they are where amateur players earn their rankings. Everyone starts out as a D player—a pure beginner. Then you work your way through the C ranks, to the Bs, and finally to the As.

As an A player, you should get opportunities to play in qualifying tournaments. These can be private regional tournaments or official state tournaments.

I remember my first state tournament. There was so much on the line. I knew that the winner qualified for an at-large bid at one of the Women's Professional Billiard Association (WPBA) events. Of course, I wasn't ready for the tournament. Everybody said I would get blown away, and they had good reason for saying it. I had been playing for only about a year, and I still didn't have much in the way of cue-ball control. Or self-control. What I did have was my confidence, and an uncanny knack for drilling difficult shots.

I fought my way to the finals, and there my inexperience was exposed. I came in second and rode the long, slow train back to Manhattan, berating myself the whole time. I figured the door had closed on me, and I wondered if I would ever get another shot at the big time.

The next day I got a call from the WPBA office. Turns out the woman who beat me couldn't make the tournament in Milwaukee. The at-large bid was mine!

After that, I don't know what came over me. I felt a surge of confidence that I had never known before. You might think I would have been happy just to have made the tour, but I wasn't. Getting on the tour just made me hungrier. Now I wanted to win, and win big.

But Milwaukee didn't go so well.

I was the youngest woman on the tour, the only Asian, and the only player from New York City.

I had brought my finest black clothes, and I made sure my makeup was perfect for the big first night. Let's just say I stood out a little bit.

A reporter from the *New York Times Magazine* was there covering the rise of the women's league. She came over to me a few times during the course of the weekend, and we talked. She didn't have a tape recorder, and she never took a single note. I thought we were chatting.

Wrong. I ended up as a big part of the article, and the portrait wasn't anything I wanted to show my mother. She called me "a bad Bond girl," painted me as a hard-drinking hussy, and claimed I wore leather and lace. None of it was true, but it didn't matter.

The women who had built the tour from scratch were enraged. They had carefully crafted an image for the tour, and now they thought I was ruining it. Plus, I was quoted in the article as saying I wanted to become number one, which some of the players thought was arrogant. But that was everyone's goal—why else would they be there?

So I was a marked woman. I had played well enough in Milwaukee to stay on the tour, but I was winning no popularity contests with the other women.

In addition to accusing me of sharking, the other players harassed me over the dress code because they thought my clothes were too sexy. My pants were tight, my shoulders were bare, and you could see lots of skin. They thought my outfits degraded the image of women's pool, but my attitude was, I'm a woman, why not dress like one? Instead of wearing blouses and slacks like they did, I kept up with New York fashion. I was listed as best-dressed in all the billiard magazines, but somehow the other players decided I was dressing improperly.

They got on me for everything. They said I made faces to try to intimidate opponents. Please. This game is hard enough without me worrying about furrowing my brow menacingly. I was just a focused player, and I wasn't born with a hangdog look. When I get serious, I look fierce.

That first year was a confusing time for me. I had wanted this so badly for so long, been so desperate to play with these women. I had worshiped them from afar, and now they were treating me like dirt. Month after month, I cried every night of every tournament. Not in front of anyone, but alone in my room. I called my old, true friends back in New York City, and they told me to hang in there. So many nights I wanted to quit the tour and just play pool for the love of the game, but I never did it.

I tried to understand the other players' perspective. I was getting more media attention than anyone else, and that bothered them. I figured that if I was a hardworking lawyer in an established firm and some young hotshot came in and got all the best accounts, I would be pretty riled, too. That's how it goes when you put forty-eight highly competitive women in a room and tell them all to go after the same prize. They're not all going to wind up holding hands and kissing cheeks.

On the other hand, I wish they had realized that I was helping our sport. Every town we went to, we suddenly got better play in the papers and the magazines. Television news crews started coming out to watch us. We were a phenomenon.

Of course, no one wanted to give me any credit for that. I was an outsider, a rebel, a troublemaker. And all I had wanted in the first place was to fit in.

It wasn't until after I gave up trying to fit in and please everyone, long after the disaster at the World Championships in Germany, that I started to feel more comfortable on the tour.

I knew I could play, and I started to show the women that I was there to stay. They could hate me if they wanted to, but they couldn't break my back.

I think that gained me a measure of respect.

Now I'm friends with a lot of the women on the tour. I've done exhibitions with Vivian Villarreal, the Texas Tornado, and photo shoots with Ewa Mataya Laurance.

The other women say I have changed. I think they've just gotten to know me better, because I never did give up, and I kept interacting with them, tournament after tournament. Maybe I don't have as big a chip on my shoulder as I did at twenty-three, but I'm still no shrinking violet. I'm there to win, and I'll destroy anyone who gets in my way. It's not the sweetest attitude, but sweetness doesn't win tournaments. You can bet that the other champions have just as much of an assassin's mentality, only they hide it better.

Thing is, I'm not ashamed of it. When I'm at the table, I'm a cold-blooded killer.

I think they mistook my demeanor at the table for my entire personality. I am actually very lighthearted when it comes to my personal life. I give huge chunks of my time and my money to charities, particularly the Scoliosis Association. I carry around magic tricks in my suitcase to entertain children in airports.

It's easy to judge me just by what you see when I'm playing. And it's easy to hate a woman who doesn't bother to smile while she's ripping your heart out. But there is more to me than that.

Even my confidence has been hard-won. Today I walk into tournaments with confidence streaming off me in energy waves. People think I must be strong, brave, and self-assured.

At that moment, I am. But there are darker moments when I question why I am even alive. For years, I had nightmares every night. I still live in terror that my opportunities will disappear suddenly, and that I will be left with nothing to show for all my work.

I have to make an effort every day to keep my attitude where I need it to be, because I know that you can decide whether you are going to be happy or sad at any moment. You can think of yourself as a winner or a loser. The scary thing is, you become what you think you are.

If you think you are a loser, you can bet that's what you will be, sooner or later. If you think you are a winner, you will become one.

Losers don't like to believe this theory. They are not ready to blame themselves for their own predicaments. It is easy for a winner to take credit for a winning attitude. For a loser to do the same takes tremendous courage, because it means it is time for him to change the way he views himself.

I wake up every morning now and bring myself around to a positive attitude. It doesn't matter if I haven't gotten enough sleep or if I'm desperate for a cup of coffee to feel human. Circumstances are just that—circumstances. You can't control them. But you can control what you think and how you feel about them. Events may spiral out of your control, but you can always determine how you'll react to them.

So wake up and tell yourself that you are going to have a good day. You are going to get things done. That way, you can walk into the poolroom dripping with the confidence you need to win.

And if you win often enough, I'll be seeing you on tour. I have made it a practice to always meet and greet every rookie at her first event. I might even buy her a cup of coffee. It's my way of helping smooth her transition to the tour, to make her life a little easier than mine was when I first joined. So what'll it be? A mocha latte? Cream, no sugar? Think about it. I'll be here.

MATCH PREPARATION

You would not believe how many pool matches are won and lost before the games even begin.

Not because the matches are fixed or because one player is obviously better than the other, but simply because only one player knew how to prepare properly.

Many players ignore this aspect of the game, but they do so at their own peril. Imagine a basketball player who just shows up for the tip-off. No stretching, no warm-ups, nothing. There is just no way he's going to play his game.

It's the same thing in pool. You need your warm-up time.

The first thing you want to do when you arrive at a tournament site is to learn all the logistical details, like where you'll be playing and when. Don't be like that Olympic sprinter who trained for four years, then missed the start time of his race.

You snooze, you lose. No one is going to hold your hand or call you up when it's time to play. It's your responsibility to know the schedule. Otherwise, you'll find yourself making excuses instead of making shots.

Once you've established your schedule, take a good, long look around the tournament area. Study it. Get familiar with it. It's a good idea to do this the day before the tournament starts, if that's possible. You want to have that room so thoroughly ingrained in your mind that when you leave to go to your hotel, or your apartment if it's a local event, you can close your eyes and picture the entire room, in detail.

You should be able to see in your mind's eye where the tables are, the chairs, the lights, the flowers and plants, the funny signs on the walls—anything that might catch your eye and distract you later, when you are shooting in the tournament.

You want it to be as familiar as your bedroom. When you are home in your room and you are reading or focusing on a task, do you suddenly see something out of the corner of your eye that distracts you? Unless you live in a roach-infested apartment, the answer is probably no. That is because you are familiar with your surroundings. A poster or a painting that's been hanging there for years is not going to suddenly demand your attention.

So really let your mind absorb the room. Take some time. The more clearly you can picture the place with your eyes closed and recognize all the landmarks, the less likely you are to become distracted during your match.

Because the truth is, no matter how much you try to help it, when you are down on a shot, your eyes will glance up. They are drawn to new phenomena—that's the way our perceptive system works. This is a good thing for survival: it's important to see the truck that wasn't there a second ago that's about to run you over, or the lion that just appeared ten feet away. It's not that helpful, though, when you are trying to shoot pool.

That is why I always try to minimize the number of new elements in my field of vision. You may still hear someone talking a few tables over, or see someone wearing a shirt you like, but at least you've made an effort to keep those distractions to a minimum.

Let that room be the last thing you see before you go to sleep the night before the tournament.

Do not waste time thinking about who you will be playing in the first, second, or third round. I know this is difficult to do. Pool is a competitive game, and you want to beat your opponent.

But here's the thing: the way to beat your opponent is to play the very best pool you can play. That is what you should focus on— playing your best and winning the tournament. It does not matter who is standing in your way. The other players almost don't exist. Except for when she makes excellent defensive shots, very little your opponent does can impact your game. She cannot block your shots or push you off balance when you are getting ready to shoot.

The truth is, you are playing against yourself. Unfortunately, as we all know, our selves can be very formidable enemies.

Consider this: What do you gain by thinking about your opponent? If you're upset because you believe that she is unbeatable, you will get a bad night's sleep and then enter the tournament with no confidence, and the combination of exhaustion and nervousness will leave you with no chance of winning.

If, on the other hand, you think, "Oh, I'm going to drill her, she's a chump," you will be overconfident. Then you will run the risk of looking past your first match, which could cause you to lose to this woman you've declared a chump. And what would that make you?

So focus on yourself, on getting your head right, and go to bed feeling invincible. Because then it truly does not matter who you are playing.

All right, then. You've slept well, you've got the place memorized. What do you do on the day of the match?

Eat well. I never eat within two hours of my match. I do eat a good-sized meal, though, four hours before it. I go for light fare, like chicken, pasta, or fish. That way, I am neither full nor hungry during a match.

I am careful about this, because after I eat I feel sluggish. Who wants to be tired and sleepy when it is time to play for money? Not me.

I want to be alert. I don't want my body wasting its energy digesting my meal, and I don't want all my blood gathering in my stomach. I need my eyes to be sharp, and my brain fresh.

This may be too much information, but I also recommend that

you use the bathroom before your match. You don't want to be distracted or uncomfortable.

Sometimes I'll be scheduled to play back-to-back matches. On those days, I'll carry some food in my purse. Not a steak—I save those for after I win the tournament. I will carry a banana or an energy bar, maybe a bagel for carbohydrates. Just enough so I won't be hungry, but not so much that I'm full.

Some players will tell you they play better with a little liquor in them. That may be true. One drink can loosen you up if you have a tight stroke. But the effects wear off very quickly, and the answer is not to take a second drink. It just doesn't feel the same; you'll start to lose your focus, aim, and coordination.

The real reason players rely on alcohol, I think, is to get confidence. That is a little pathetic, though, and certainly not good for you in the long run. Liquid confidence is a poor substitute for the real thing, which is earned through practice and studying the game.

Okay. The pregame meal is done, and the match is fast approaching. Your palms are sweaty and your heart is in your throat.

What I do then is get away from everyone. If I don't have time to go back to my hotel room, I will find a bathroom. Honestly. I will find a stall and sit on the toilet and just think about how much I love this game.

I will picture every possible scenario in my mind, and then envision how I will come out a winner. I may picture myself just stomping an opponent. Or imagine myself squandering a big lead and being forced to make a tough shot to win. Or I'll see my opponent charging ahead, and then see myself coming back, roaring through her like it was nothing.

Picture all the possibilities, and picture how strongly you are going to come through.

I think about how I look at the table when I am playing my best. Solid. Confident. Powerful.

I picture the faces in the crowd, jaws just dropping. I see myself facing a tough lie, picture my opponent on the edge of her seat, chalk in hand, and I see the shot go in, and in my mind's eye, I don't even have to look over—she's slumping in her seat, defeated.

After that, when I walk into the tournament arena, there is nothing but confidence pouring off me. It's obvious to everyone in the room—the crowd, the workers at the poolroom, and my opponents. They all know I've come to play. You can't tell me that doesn't provide an advantage before the match even starts.

Half an hour before the match, I will start working out my eyes. Never, ever—*ever*—warm-up shooting tough shots just before a match. It's suicide. You try them, you miss a few, and you start telling yourself, "Oh no. I'm not playing well."

Once that voice kicks in, you've lost the edge you worked so hard to gain. So shoot easy shots and feel the balls going in, one after the other.

Get your eyes moving; let them focus on the edges of the balls. When your opponent takes her turn at the table, keep exercising your eyes. Look at bright colors around the room. Focus on strong, solid, matte colors. Avoid looking directly at bright lights. They have the same disorienting effect as a flashbulb on a camera, and you don't want your eyes struggling to recover and readjust; you want them perfectly focused.

Follow this routine, and you will feel just as you should before any match, no matter how big or how small. You'll be calm but pumped up. Your thinking will be clear. You will feel like a panther stalking his prey. You will be the most intimidating, calculating, meticulous work of art that you can be, and you will play the best pool of your life.

PRESENTATION COUNTS

20

Everybody knows you can't judge a book by its cover. But if you see a book with a torn, tattered cover that looks like it's been dropped in the bathtub and gone halfway through a shredder, you know one thing for sure: its owner didn't care enough about that book to keep it looking good.

Your clothes are your cover. They say a lot about you, because they are something that is totally within your control. You chose them. You make a statement with them, whether you want to or not. You cannot decide the shape of your face or the sound of your voice, but you make a decision, every day, as to what side of yourself you are going to show the world.

So the question becomes, How much do you care about yourself? I'm not saying you have to wear a tuxedo to watch a baseball game, and I'm not about to tell you not to wear jeans or sneakers.

I'm just saying that you should make conscious choices every day about what you wear and how you look. It makes an incredible difference in the way you are perceived. If you don't believe me, go out one night looking like a total slob. Leave your shirt untucked, your hair knotted, and your shoes untied. Are you getting a lot of positive attention? Do you feel good about yourself, or are you insecure?

Now pick another night and go out looking your best. If you are a woman, get your hair styled and your nails done. If you're a guy, get a good close shave and put on your best cologne. Wear your nicest clothes, even if they are just a little too fancy for wherever you're going.

How does that feel? Powerful, right? Because you're in command. You've shown everyone in the room, including yourself, that you know how to take care of yourself, and that you're worth it.

I think those may be the two most important messages you can convey. First, that you've got your act together and, second, that you know you are worth being cared for and attended to.

In contrast, slobs send out the message that the world has won.

Now think about this in terms of pool.

If a guy walks in with his pants falling down and he's got two and a half days' worth of stubble crawling out of his cheekbones, is he going to inspire confidence? Is he going to be capable of intimidating his opponent? I don't think so. Pool is all about precision, and if this guy can't even find a belt, or pants that fit, how is he going to think ahead three shots?

When I walk into a poolroom for a tournament, I want everything to be perfect, from head to toe. My hair will be clean and shiny, my nails freshly painted, my makeup done. I wear black designer clothes, and they will never be wrinkled or rumpled.

I want everyone to know that I was up earlier than they were, preparing for my match. It is my way of showing them that I am more ready than they are for the challenge at hand. It shows that I am in complete control, and that I think highly enough of myself to present the best me I can to my opponent, the fans, and the television cameras.

This tactic works in every arena, not just in poolrooms. The businessman with the crisp suit and elegant knotted tie has an innate advantage over the man who looks like he just rolled out of bed. It doesn't mean he will win the negotiations every time, just as a Givenchy dress doesn't guarantee success at the pool table, but it gives him an unmistakable edge.

In a game that is 90 percent mental, that edge may be all you need.

At times, I have gone overboard.

When I was growing up my family never had a lot of money, and I wore a lot of hand-me-downs and discount outfits. Maybe it's crazy, but as a girl I always felt a tinge of shame and jealousy when I saw women with beautiful clothing and jewelry. They seemed so majestic, so captivating. And men who knew how to dress always struck me as rare and sexy.

So when I started winning tournaments, I started buying expensive clothes. It was the first big money I had ever seen, and for a while I assumed it would last forever.

The pool magazines quickly named me the best-dressed and most charismatic player on the tour.

But that didn't make me relax. When I read those clippings, I felt I had to justify them. It is one of my weakest points that I cannot accept success more graciously. Success always makes me think that failure must be lurking right around the corner.

I didn't want to be exposed as a woman with just one or two nice outfits, not the fancy dresser that everyone thought I was. So I bought more. And more.

And I didn't even look at the price tags.

I spent $50,000 on clothes in one year.

I tried calling the IRS to see if I could take it off my taxes as a business expense, but they just laughed. Technically, my clothing is a uniform, but they said it just didn't qualify!

At a couple of tournaments, the women on the rules committee sent me back to my hotel to slip into something a little less comfortable. Which I think is ridiculous.

It really showed me the difference between playing against men and against women. Both sexes can be fierce competitors, but there is a difference between a catfight and a dogfight.

Back at Chelsea Billiards, the guys were just as petty—they were backstabbing hustlers and they had inane squabbles all the time. But the fights were always about the game. It was all about who matched up with who, who was the best player, who had picked out a sucker first. Your personality never really entered into the debate—it was much more concrete.

The tour was a much trickier affair. There I cared about whether the other women liked me. There were tons of cliques; at Chelsea, it was every man and woman for him- or herself. With the cliques came feelings of alienation. It was harder for me, and it evoked my insecurities, because it was no longer about measurable skills—it was about my personality. Whereas the men judged my stroke, the women judged my soul.

Not to mention my shoes.

I would have understood the women's fashion gripes if I had even once heard a fan complain about anything I wore being too risqué. But only the other players criticized my catsuits and sleeveless outfits with spaghetti straps. I would never wear anything slutty anyway. It's not my style, and besides, I know that there are youngsters at all our matches.

I consider myself a good girl, and there's no way I'm going to send out the wrong message to a child, or make her parents feel like they shouldn't bring her to see my matches.

By now, things have sort of settled down on the clothing front. I still bend the rules, but I try not to break them. I still like nice clothes, but I have made a promise to my husband to at least look at the price tag before I buy anything. It hasn't stopped me too often, but at least I am conscious of what I am spending, and that helps me make better, more informed decisions.

Even today, though, there is no chance you'll catch me at a tournament with my hair a mess and my face looking like I just woke up. I just don't feel good doing that. So for as long as I'm playing, expect to see me in tight-fitting black outfits. If you come to the tournament and snag a front-row seat, you'll be smelling my favorite perfume.

Because when I look good, I feel good, and when I feel good, I play great pool.

BALANCING A CAREER AND A FAMILY

They say it's common knowledge that when two pool players get married, both their games go to hell.

Since I married George Breedlove, in 1996, I've dropped from number one to number two in the world, and he's left professional pool completely, so on the surface, it sure looks like we back that statement up.

But I don't think it's true. George left pool because the men's game is in a sorry state, with few sponsors, no television exposure, and almost no fans. He's built up his own outdoor-furniture business, and he's doing well.

As for me, I have slipped a little, but not because of George. Over the last three years, my ailments have gotten worse, and I have been in constant pain, so I can't practice as much as I'd like to. With the other professionals getting better all the time, it is tougher than ever to take home tournament wins.

In truth, though, George has helped me and my game far more than our marriage has hurt it. He has always been there, as a friend, a lover, and a supportive husband. When I win, he celebrates with me, and when I lose, he stands by me.

And I'm not so easy to be around when I lose. I used to beat myself up for days, wondering what I did wrong and how I could fix it. I would get irritable, and nobody would want to spend more than five minutes by my side. But George played the game, and he knows how to console me. After a tough match, we'll just walk through the streets in silence, catch a movie, or head back to our room and eat

all the candy out of the hotel minibar. Because really, there's nothing you can say to a good pool player who has just lost a match. "Nice try" just doesn't get it done.

All you can do is hang in there and feel what your partner is feeling. That's what George does. He'll stay in that moment with me until I am ready to scream or cry. Then, when the time is right, he'll do something to make me laugh. It can be a joke, or a funny face, or just a look. And once I am laughing, we both know that there's another tournament next month, and that everything will be all right in the end.

That is not to say that marriage has been easy. I don't think there is such a thing as an easy marriage. It's especially hard when one partner has to be on the road as often as I am—not just for tournaments but for exhibitions, speeches, and charity functions.

So last year George and I made a deal. We promised never to be apart for more than seven days. It has helped us tremendously. It is easy to minimize a relationship, to put it in a corner of your mind and say it doesn't matter, just because you don't want to miss that person, or wonder what they're doing while you're gone.

We are extremely committed to our marriage, and we don't want to drift apart while I'm away on tour. So we make a real effort to keep in touch with each other, and to keep our marriage alive in our hearts even when we're apart. I call him every day, no matter if I'm in Toledo or Taipei.

Sometimes it's nice just to hear his voice.

We make sure that when we're home in Indianapolis we spend real time together. We love hanging out with the neighborhood kids, watching the Pacers, taking walks, and going out to dinner. It seems like every date affirms our connection.

So many people I know never go for dates with their spouse. They just kind of hang out every night. Which is nice sometimes, but I think going out and doing things keeps life more interesting. And I could be wrong, but I think a boring marriage is a marriage headed for trouble.

George and I don't have any children. This makes me sad, because there is nothing I want more than to raise a family. Unfortunately, my doctors have told me that for now I am too weak to carry a baby to term. My back simply would not be able to take the strain.

We have thought about adopting, but I really want to experience the entire process, from beginning to end, inside my body. The doctors have told me that I could have surgery to replace the rod in my back with an updated rod. If I went through with it, in a few years I would probably be strong enough to become a mother.

The problem is that during my rehabilitation, I would not be able to practice enough to keep my competitive form. I don't honestly know what I would do if I couldn't play pool for that long. As it is, I go crazy if I can't play for two days. The game is so intertwined with my life and my identity that I'm not sure who I would be without it.

It would mean giving up my career in my prime, sacrificing my best professional years to spend them rehabilitating my back. For now, I cannot bring myself to do that. Financially, I couldn't afford it. Mentally and spiritually, I cannot imagine a life without this game.

Thankfully, I am young. I can play for a while longer and still have the surgery in time to raise a healthy family.

For now, this looks like the best option. Of course, this means I will still have to walk away from the game at a young age, but there comes a time when different things gain more importance.

I care too much about children never to have at least one of my own. Every time I see a child, my heart flutters. I want to feed them, dress them, take them for walks in the park.

George has two daughters, Morgan and Olivia, from a previous marriage, and I adore them. We hang out together all the time. But sometimes after they're gone, it makes me realize all the more how difficult the choices before me are.

So I will wait to be a mother. For now, I am still learning how to be a wife. When I go on the road, I am treated like a celebrity. I'm the Black Widow, and the people who have paid for me to visit them are glad I am there. I put on a good show, and they pay me well. They take care of everything I need.

When I get home, though, I'm not the Black Widow anymore. I'm Jeanette, George Breedlove's wife. He doesn't have to get up and get the butter for me just because I want him to.

I have to keep in mind who I really am in order to keep sanity around the house. I have to readjust to the real life of Jeanette Lee Breedlove, who likes playing one-on-one basketball with her husband in the driveway, who likes cooking for her man, and even treating him to late-night foot massages.

It's funny. I thought I was going to talk about how to balance a career and a family, but I realized it's just the opposite. It's the career and the marriage that balance me. Together they keep me sane, and make me into a whole person.

And that's the goal of life, in the end, isn't it?

22 DEALING WITH FAME

§ The first time I was recognized on the street, I was about twenty-two years old.

I wasn't dressed up. I had on a black T-shirt and jeans. My hair was in a ponytail, and I didn't have my cue stick with me. I was certainly no celebrity, and I wasn't dolled up like a glamour girl.

I was just running to the deli near SoHo Billiards to pick up a turkey sandwich and a Coke.

"Hey, aren't you Jeanette Lee?" asked a guy leaving the store as I entered. "Aren't you the Black Widow?"

I smiled so wide I'm surprised my teeth didn't crack.

I couldn't believe that somebody actually knew who I was. I hardly knew who I was back then.

And here I was, being recognized for my talent! That was the best part of it, for me. For that second, I felt like I was part of an elite group. That felt too cool. I could tell from the look on his face that this guy actually admired me.

After all my years of admiring and worshiping other people, it was a total rush. I had always looked up to the people around me, envied their hairstyles, their fashionable clothes, and their knowledge of the world. I would try to hang out with my sister's friends, and I was always awed by how much they knew. They knew how to work hard and how to study, and they could discuss music and art and history and I would just sit there and grunt and feel like an idiot.

I had always felt so far below everybody, and here was this man, a total stranger, looking up to me!

I ran back to the poolroom and told all my friends.

But soon after that rush of excitement, I developed a feeling of responsibility. As I played in more and more tournaments, I became more aware of the crowds. Fans started asking for my autograph.

The first time that happened, I assured the guy he didn't want it.

"I'm not really one of them," I said.

"Aren't you playing?" he asked.

"Well, yeah, but . . ."

He made me sign. And it was so uncomfortable I can't even tell you. Because I wasn't prepared for it at all. It seemed like somehow by signing his poster, I was declaring to the world that I was somebody. And after all those years of being nobody, I really wasn't convinced.

I signed though, and then I looked at him and he looked at me and I looked back down at the poster and said, "My God, I've got an ugly autograph."

He smiled and walked away, but the whole encounter didn't

leave me with a great feeling. It was scary. I had felt so badly about myself my entire life, and now that I had arrived, instead of feeling good about myself and saying, "Wow, they respect me and I deserve it," I was thinking, "What if they find out I'm really not worth it?"

I felt like an imposter. Why would anyone want my name on anything, I wondered. I'm no better or different than they are.

And yet part of me enjoyed the attention. Suddenly everyone was patting me on the back, asking how I was doing, wondering if they could do anything for me. Before, I had been even less than a fly on the wall—more like a fly's wing splattered against the wall—and now, suddenly, I was a star.

I had a hard time adapting. My responsibility turned to feelings of guilt. Every time I won any money at a tournament, I would send huge chunks of it to my family. I wasn't a multimillionaire or anything, but I felt like I had to do something for them. After a while, though, I felt like buying them gifts wasn't enough. I started a fund for my cousins, so that they would be able to go to college when the time came.

I also started doing a lot of charity work. I became a spokeswoman for the Scoliosis Association, participated in fund-raisers for various charities such as the Boys and Girls Club, joined the Diverse Races Committee for the Women's Sports Foundation, and started the Jeanette Lee Foundation, a philanthropic organization dedicated to helping children live better lives.

Even so, I still felt somewhat guilty about my success. When you come from a background with no money and not too much hope, there is always this sense that you turned your back on people.

So I started doing everything I could to make myself feel better. I took new professional players under my wing, taught them how to market themselves, arranged for them to get top-level sponsors.

I became the best friend anyone could ever have. Guests were always welcome at my house, and I would drive them all over town whenever they needed to go anywhere.

Eventually, though, all this extracurricular activity cut into my practice time. I tried to meet every demand, but I wasn't taking care of the most important thing: my game.

When tournament time came, I invariably placed second or third. And then all those friends who I had been chauffeuring and playing hostess for would ask, What's the matter, Jeanette? Aren't you practicing? It started driving me nuts. Because I'm not the type of person content to place second. It's just not in my nature.

So I started saying no to people. I wasn't doing it to hurt anyone, and I felt brutal, but I had to get my stuff done. I could give only so much of my time and energy and still be happy and successful. And so I learned to set limits, and to make sure that I got the time I needed for practicing at the table.

And soon I was back on top.

I'm still wrestling with how to handle fans. Ninety-eight percent of the time, I'll go above and beyond. If they want my autograph, I'll give it to them, and I'll even offer to carry their posters around to other top players, so everyone can sign.

I give away key chains to our youngest fans and do magic tricks for the others. At the charity event we always hold on the night before the tournament starts, I'll include fans in my trick shots. People can send things to my office with a self-addressed, stamped envelope, and I'll sign whatever they want. When I meet fans at the matches, I'll look them in the eye, shake their hand, and take a little time to talk with them, or get in a picture if they want.

But there are times, like right before a match, when I have learned to say no. Not because I'm in a bad mood but because I know how important it is to stay focused before a match, and how easy it is to become distracted.

I used to feel really bad about this. I'd tell myself that they paid $20 to come see me play; it's the least I could do. But then I realized that I paid $2,000 to come to town and play, and that my entire salary depends on my performance at these events.

So even though I try to be understanding and I try to be as nice as possible, sometimes I wish people would just accept that there is a time and a place for everything.

If that's not sweet enough, I'm sorry. Deal with it.

Some people can't. A couple of years ago, I was entered in a huge tournament for professionals and amateurs in Valley Forge, Pennsylvania. I had to play four matches in a row before I got an hour-and-a-half lunch break, with more matches to follow in the afternoon.

By the time my first four matches were over, I was starving. I slipped out with a friend, who drove me fifteen miles to an out-of-the-way diner, where we could enjoy some air-conditioned peace and quiet.

I ordered a soup and salad, and it came promptly. But before I could bring the spoon to my lips, three guys barged in and bounded over to our table.

"Sorry," said one of them. "But I was worried I couldn't get your autograph at the arena, so we followed you here."

The spoon was still halfway to my mouth, and I looked at him incredulously.

I signed quickly, and he said, "I have just a few questions I'm dying to ask you."

I should have told him to read this book, had I known then that it would be coming out. Instead, I sat there like a hostage and answered his questions: When did you get started? How do you practice? Why do they call you the Black Widow?

Then I looked at him and said, "Look, I'm really sorry, but I've got matches to play this afternoon, and I really need this time to relax."

"Oh sure, I understand completely," he said. "No problem. I've only got a few more questions."

That is just one incident out of hundreds.

I have had people follow me to my hotel; I've had them knock on the door to my room. I have had strangers send me flowers and teddy bears—which I actually don't mind. If you get a bouquet of flowers, that's sweet. If you get a bouquet every month for a year, that's a little scary.

I have always managed to fend off stalkers by approaching them directly. I don't know if it's the force of my personality that deters them, but I've found that if you talk directly to someone like a human being, they can't turn you into some sort of twisted fantasy.

Of course, some people are just incorrigible. I was seated on the toilet at a tournament last year when suddenly somebody slipped a tour program underneath the stall and asked me to sign it!

It was a woman who said she was doing it for a man, who had decided it would have been inappropriate for him to come into the women's room and approach me himself. Nice to know he has a firm sense of decency.

So there I was, this supposedly famous person, caged like an animal in the most private moment imaginable, signing an autograph in a bathroom stall.

23 NO EXCUSES

So many times, I'll be getting ready to play someone and they'll start in with a series of potential excuses—before we've even started!

They'll say that they're hungry, or tired, or haven't played in weeks. That way, no matter what happens, no matter how badly they play, they've got a built-in excuse.

Please, don't become one of these players.

If you remember just one thing from this book, let it be the courage to go out, play your best, and accept the results.

Everyone can find an excuse. It takes a brave person to face reality without a crutch. I don't sit around feeling sorry for myself. Instead, I do everything I can to gain that number one ranking back. I work out. I eat right. I try to stretch my back whenever I can. I practice all the time.

And I don't make excuses.

I remember when the pain really started getting to me, back in 1997. I was playing in a tournament, and when I bent down to shoot, I experienced true agony. I saw four balls where there was only one. I was on the verge of tears, terrified that I would make a fool of myself because I could not even see straight.

You cannot imagine my frustration. I had come so far, worked so hard to become number one, but right then I saw it all slipping away.

I walked over to my husband, who was in the stands watching.

"George, I can't do this," I said.

"So what do you want to do? Quit?" he asked.

That got me mad. Of course I didn't want to quit. I'm not a quitter.

"What, are you insane?" I screamed at him. "If I have to lose I'll go in there and lose, but I'm not about to forfeit!"

"So you're gonna go in there and play?" he asked.

I nodded.

"You're gonna bend over the table and shoot this shot even though your back's hurting?"

I nodded again.

"Well, if you're going to play, and you're going to get down on that ball, shoot to make it," he said. "Those are your choices. Either you quit, you shoot to miss, or you shoot to make it."

And he was right. So many people shoot not to lose. They are preoccupied with everything that could go wrong. They are preparing excuses just in case they need them. I used to be guilty of the same thing.

But that afternoon I realized there are only two ways to play the game. You can either play to win or play to avoid losing. And from that point on, I've played to win.

Once you make that commitment, there can't be any half-stepping. It's an enormous risk, going out there and giving it your all, because if you fail, you have no excuse. You just came up short. You tried hard, but you hit your limit. That's a terrifying prospect, and that is why people come prepared with a litany of excuses. So they don't have to take true and full responsibility for what goes on, either at the table or in their lives.

I was scared that day, but I went back to the table.

And for a few minutes, I could not miss a ball. Every time I bent over, I was shaking in pain. But I focused on that object ball, on that one tiny target point, and I decided that nothing in the world was going to make me miss.

I was so determined to make that one shot, every time, just that one shot in front of me. Nothing else mattered. I didn't have to worry about winning or losing the tournament; I didn't have to worry about making a fool of myself or leaving my opponent a perfect opportunity.

Soon I cooled off. I started missing shots. Shots I might have made if I were feeling better. And in the end, I didn't win. But I had survived, and I had gained something. I knew then I would never give up, that I wouldn't use excuses, and that I would beat any handicap I had.

I didn't win another tournament for a year. I lost my number one ranking. Everybody thought I was finished, except for me. Because I knew I had a champion's heart.

I had heard everyone's excuses for their poor play, and I had lived through most of them myself. Financial problems, family crises, stress, and exhaustion. But the truth is, I remembered times when I didn't have any of these problems—days when I felt great, had nothing to worry about, slept well, and ate just the right food before the match—and still lost.

So I knew that it was all about what you brought to the table. How much of yourself you were willing to lay on the line.

And then in Dallas, in February 1999, I faced my greatest personal challenge. On the final day of the tournament, I was still alive, but I was in the loser's bracket. That meant I had lost once already, and I had to win four straight matches just to reach the finals.

Minutes before my first match of the day, my back went into spasmodic convulsions. I collapsed on the floor in front of everyone. I admit it—I bawled like a baby, writhing and shaking on the ground.

Friends tried to move me, but I asked them to please leave me alone. I could barely see, I was in so much pain, but I hated that people were staring. I was on the verge of fainting. The announcer called my match over the loudspeaker, and I had to take my fifteen-minute allowance.

I knew that if I couldn't play in fifteen minutes, I would have to forfeit for the first time in my career.

Luckily, Nesli O'Hare, a fellow pro, was there, and she had a heating pad she had borrowed from Ewa. She helped me into the bathroom, and I lay down on the floor. She plugged the pad into a socket in the bathroom wall, and I lifted my legs up onto a bench.

I swallowed eight hundred milligrams of Advil right there, gulping them down while lying on the cold tile floor.

After about twelve minutes, I stood up. The spasms had calmed down, but my entire back still ached.

I went to the table thinking only of survival.

Over and over I told myself, Survive. Shoot to win, even if you are going to lose. Normally I never even think about losing, but on that day I didn't think I had a chance. I knew it would take a miracle for me to win the tournament, so I just focused on one match at a time, one shot at a time.

I didn't make every shot. I missed shots I can normally make. But I made the shots that counted. And I won the first match. Again I took my fifteen minutes, and again I had to lie down. I won the second match, and the third match too. I beat some of the best players in the world: Line Kjoersvik of Norway, Gerda Hofstatter of Austria, and then Allison Fisher, from England.

In the final match, I played Karen Corr. I could barely look at the table. My eyes were watering on almost every shot. It was a close match right up till the end. And when I sunk that last 9-ball, I could not believe I had won.

There were a million people watching, but I didn't care. I started crying again, but these were a different kind of tears than the ones I had shed on the floor just hours before. These were tears of joy, of pride in my accomplishment, and of relief.

I passed out ten minutes later in my hotel room and slept a contented sleep.

CONCLUSION

This is where I am supposed to wrap everything up in a little bow and send you on your way, as if you were now perfectly armed and ready to conquer the world.

But I can't. If I have learned anything so far, it's that life, like pool, is not about conclusions. It's about the journey.

Don't worry so much about the destination—concentrate on how you are getting there. It is all those little moments on the way to that place that constitute life.

If you focus only on the end result, you miss everything. Don't beat yourself up if you are not a champion the day after you finish reading this book. What is important is not so much where you are going, but where you are now.

Every shot, whether you make it or miss it, is a step toward something better. Every mistake is part of a growing process. Trust that you are doing everything you can to improve.

You will probably never be satisfied with your game—I know I'm not. If that makes you miserable, you should try something else, something easier to master. If, on the other hand, that challenges you to try harder, to appreciate every step in the process of improving, then you have found a sport that you can play for life.

Pool is not like Mount Everest. There is no mountaintop, no summit to reach. There are only greater heights to strive for.

PHOTO CREDITS

Grateful acknowledgment is made to the following for permission to reproduce the photographs used herein:

Tony Clevenger   pages 45, 47, 50, 52, 53, 59, 179, 207 (top)

Michael Rudinoff   page 57

Billiards Digest   pages 66, 119, 127

Stan Shaffer   page 137

Tom Hebert   page 149

Herb Wilmot   page 167

Mike DiMotta   page 180

Jay H. Yoon   page 185

Tom Briglia   page 188

Elizabeth Malby   page 207 (bottom)

INDEX

ABOUT THE AUTHORS

Jeanette Lee went from being an unranked amateur to the number one player in the world in her first year as a professional. She's been named Sportsperson of the Year by the WPBA and Player of the Year by *Billiards Digest* and *Pool and Billiard* magazine. She lives in Indianapolis with her husband, George Breedlove. Between tournaments, she raises money for her charity, the Jeanette Lee Foundation, gives motivational speeches, and performs trick shot exhibitions. Known by her nickname, the Black Widow, Jeanette is currently the most recognized pool player in the world.

Adam Scott Gershenson was born in 1970, and he knew by kindergarten that he wanted to be a writer. Since his graduation from Columbia University's Literature Writing Program, he has written for the *New York Times, USA Today,* and Reuters. He is a reporter with the *Journal News* in Westchester, New York, and lives on Manhattan's Upper West Side.